THE HEALING
POWER
—of the—
WORD

SABRINA SURRENCY

The Healing Power of The Word
Copyright February to July 2024, Sabrina Surrency.
All Rights Reserved.

No part of this book may be reproduced or transmitted in any form or by any means, electronic or mechanical, including photocopying, recording, or by any information storage or retrieval system without the written permission of the author or the publisher, except where permitted by law.

Paperback
Hardcover
eBook

Publisher: Pink Butterfly Press LLC. Since 2019.
www.Pinkbutterflypressllc.com

Dedication

To my parents, for planting the seed
of love within me. Thanks for teaching me to
love beyond the boundaries of blood.
I am forever grateful.

Introduction

I am Sabrina, I am a mother of four mighty sons, I am the middle sister of two magnificent women, I am the daughter of a feisty 76 year old, I am a friend and confidante to many, I am the leader of an enthusiastic team of individuals on our nursing unit at the hospital (some call it work but what I do at Baptist Medical Center is a privilege), I am a nurse, I am a child of the King, I am blessed beyond measure, and I am so grateful to all whom God has blessed to cross my path. I am so thankful to God for blessing me with an opportunity to share His word and spread the good news to as many people whom He has positioned to receive.

As I sit here contemplating this exciting, path that God has placed me on, I find myself reflecting on the birth of possibilities. The daily process of me expounding on the word was birthed in the belly of a co-worker who has become a dear and well-respected friend. She started by sending the scripture of the day to a few people in her circle. God has commanded us to reach higher and greater than what we see so that we can spread the good news to the masses.

I have been blessed with an abundance of hunger, thirst, and a desire to learn more about His word and better understand it's meaning. From this desire to learn more about His word, has stemmed a desire to spread the word to as many people who are willing to read, learn, and grow in the word. I'm so appreciative to have the word so readily available to guide and direct my path. "All scripture is given by inspiration of God, and is profitable for doctrine, for reproof, for correction, for instruction in righteousness, 17. That the man of God may be complete, thoroughly equipped for every good work." Lord, thank you for equipping us for this great work. My desire if for you to get all the glory!

    I'm looking forward to blazing this path that God has allowed, predestined, and preordained just for us. Without God going before us, we will not succeed, but with God on our side, all things are possible, and our success is sure. I ask that you come along with me on this journey, join me as I place my hope and faith in God, and let's ask him to position us to experience greater as we spread the word to the masses. Our God is worthy, He's faithful, and He's true in all things. Blessings

1

Good Morning!

Then Jesus said to them again, "Most assuredly, I say to you, I am the door of the sheep. 8 All who ever came before Me are thieves and robbers, but the sheep did not hear them. 9 I am the door. If anyone enters by Me, he will be saved, and will go in and out and find pasture. **John**

To His listeners who are aware that Yahweh is the Shepherd of Israel, Jesus presents another solemn claim; "I am the good shepherd." He places Himself in contrast to Israel's religious leaders, who were supposed to be faithful shepherds, but they were more like evil false shepherds. He is also the door of the sheep not the fold. Jesus is in charge of and cares for the lives of the sheep. To emphasize the access to God He provides. He calls Himself door, without Him, no one enters the fold. Thank You Jesus for laying down Your life for such an undeserving wretch like me. We are forever grateful. Blessings

2 Good Morning!

Jesus said to her, "I am the resurrection and the life. He who believes in Me, though he may die, he shall live. 26 And whoever lives and believes in Me shall never die. Do you believe this?" **John**

Mary is familiar with the Old Testament teaching on the resurrection. Jesus' additional revelation concerns His identity as the One who raises the dead, who guarantees that those who believe in Him May die physically, but it will not last forever. Physical death will be openly and finally defeated at the future resurrection. Lazarus being raised from the dead was a foreshadowing of this great event that's yet to come. Thank you Lord for the resurrection, we believe. Blessings

3

Good Morning!

Then Jesus said to them again, "Most assuredly, I say to you, I am the door of the sheep. 8 All who ever came before Me are thieves and robbers, but the sheep did not hear them. 9 I am the door. If anyone enters by Me, he will be saved, and will go in and out and find pasture. **John**

To His listeners who are aware that Yahweh is the Shepherd of Israel, Jesus presents another solemn claim; "I am the good shepherd." He places Himself in contrast to Israel's religious leaders, who were supposed to be faithful shepherds, but they were more like evil false shepherds. He is also the door of the sheep not the fold. Jesus is in charge of and cares for the lives of the sheep. To emphasize the access to God He provides. He calls Himself door, without Him, no one enters the fold. Thank You Jesus for laying down Your life for such an undeserving wretch like me. We are forever grateful. Blessings

4 Good Morning!

For the grace of God that brings salvation has appeared to all men, 12 teaching us that, denying ungodliness and worldly lusts, we should live soberly, righteously, and godly in the present age. **Titus**

All men have an opportunity to accept the call of our Lord and Savior so that we can experience everlasting life. In order to be positioned and taught to live a life where we can deny ungodliness and the lusts of this world, we must strive to be clear headed, upright, humble and righteous in the eyes of God. In the Bible, we have numerous godly rules and important instructions on how to live right. We thank God for the word that educates believers in sound doctrine, purity of heart, and saintly behavior. So as we journey through the ups and downs of life, we are reminded that we need to implement these rules for living righteously before all men because we want God to be pleased with us at all times. Be encouraged. Blessings

5 Good Morning!

But the Lord is faithful, who will establish you and guard you from the evil one.
II Thessalonians

We serve a God who cannot lie, He cannot twist the truth, nor can He change His promises up based on our negative or erratic behaviors. If our God said it, it's coming to pass. Many of us have clearly heard the voice of God, He used someone to speak into your life, or He has given you a vision of better days to come, but you're looking at your current situation or circumstance and you're wondering if it was really God who made the promises because it looks like the enemy is winning. We come to encourage you on this day and remind you that we can be totally confident in our God's abilities. So, we can trust Him to strengthen us, firmly establish us, and protect us from the tricks and plans of the enemy. Because of His faithfulness, He will not allow evil people to gain a victory over any believer. If God has promised you that better is coming, hold on to what He said, He's already strengthened you for the journey, He equipped you before you were formed in your mother's womb for the process, so as He establishes you to receive the promise keep your eyes on Him because it has to come to pass. You're closer today than you were on yesterday, don't give up on His promises. Be encouraged. Blessings

6 Good Morning!

When I consider Your heavens, the work of Your fingers, The moon and the stars, which You have ordained, 4 What is man that You are mindful of him, And the son of man that You visit him? **Psalms**

In this psalm David reflects on God's majesty that is displayed in the creation. The heavens declare God's glory. Against the backdrop of this glory, man seems insignificant, but God chose man to rule the earth, He chose man to be a little lower than the angels, He chose man to have dominion over all of His creatures. By giving us this awesome responsibility, God has crowned us with His glory and honor. We are grateful to our loving Father, for all that He has done for us. Blessings

7 Good Morning!

Oh, give thanks to the Lord, for He is good!
For His mercy endures forever.
I Chronicles

God's love is relentless, immeasurable, and ever ending... it can endure and persevere through absolutely anything! He is our forever God who is filled with forever love! Since His love is steadfast and enduring, it means that He will never give up on us so don't be fooled by the trick of the enemy. The enemy will bring our transgressions back to our remembrance and make us think we need to repent again. Our God is such a loving, gracious, and forgiving God we are so thankful and so grateful that He has promised to never leave us nor forsake us. Blessings

8 Good Morning!

Be sober, be vigilant; because your adversary the devil walks about like a roaring lion, seeking whom he may devour. 9 Resist him, steadfast in the faith, knowing that the same sufferings are experienced by your brotherhood in the world. **I Peter**

Christians must be sober and watchful, responding to satanic opposition with faith and firm resistance. We have to boldly resist the enemy in faith because his attacks are spiritual, but the wounds are manifested in the natural.. jealousy, envy, doubt, negativity, anger, hatred, anxiety, fear, etc.. we are not alone in this spiritual fight, the battle has already been won, but we often fight as if this were a new battle. When the enemy attacks, we must fight in faith because our faith will reflect His love, His love will overcome and overshadow every obstacle in our path, when His love overshadows, His Spirit tears down strongholds that have woven themselves into the natural realm to stage the attacks. Trust God, the enemy doesn't stand a chance against Him. Be encouraged. Blessings

9 *Good Morning!*

For I am not ashamed of the gospel of Christ, for it is the power of God to salvation for everyone who believes, for the Jew first and also for the Greek. **Romans**

The gospel is a good message. The essential facts of the gospel include the incarnation of the Son of God, His atoning death on the cross for our sins, His victorious resurrection for our justification, and the promise of His return for His people. We can make it even more plain, in 1 Corinthians 15:3, we find the clearest an most concise essence of the gospel.. Christ died for our sins, He was buried, He rose again on the third day, and He was seen by many eyewitnesses. We are calling all who have accepted Christ as their Lord and Savior to show others how to respond to the truths of the good message in repentance and faith. We are living in a time where those who don't know Christ need to not only hear the word of God spoken, but they need to see the sermon of our lives daily. Are you striving to live a life that's pleasing to God so that He can draw men unto Him? And no, your life doesn't have to be perfect, but when you fall, what does your sermon look like? Many of the witnesses fell in the Bible. Be encouraged. Blessings

10 *Good Morning!*

But this I say: He who sows sparingly will also reap sparingly, and he who sows bountifully will also reap bountifully. **II Corinthians**

God operates through a covenant of trust, which demands our faithfulness. God is our redeemer and He seeks a relationship of mutuality and honesty with us. When Paul tells us, the person who sows sparingly will reap sparingly, he is not suggesting that God will not give us good things until we give Him good things, it is a direct pronouncement of God's actions towards our stinginess and our selfishness. It is a truth, a real practical result of what happens when we do not put enough seed into the ground. Let's strive to sow seeds of positivity, growth, and love, seeds that will produce a bounty of good fruit and an abundance of it. We are grateful. Blessings

11 Good Morning!

You are of God, little children, and have overcome them, because He who is in you is greater than he who is in the world. **I John**

Greater is He that is within me than he that is in the world. Thank God for the Holy Spirit who lives in us. We have overcome by the blood of the Lamb and we are grateful. God cares for those of us who trust in Him, this will assure us the victory over the enemy because He lives on the inside of us. All glory to God. Blessings

12 *Good Morning!*

Therefore I take pleasure in infirmities, in reproaches, in needs, in persecutions, in distresses, for Christ's sake. For when I am weak, then I am strong. **II Corinthians**

In order for us to go through and come out triumphantly, we need to go in with an attitude of strength and determination. We serve a God who shows us favor, teaches us how to be honorable, and humble and He covers us with His loving grace and mercy. When we have done all that we can do to stand, God steps in to be the source of strength that He has promised to be each and every time the need arises. Thank You Lord for being strong when we are at our lowest and experiencing weaknesses only You can conquer. We are grateful. Blessings

13 Good Morning!

For God did not send His Son into the world to condemn the world, but that the world through Him might be saved. **John**

When a man is confronted with Jesus, his soul responds to the wonder and beauty of Him, he is on his way to salvation. But if, when he is confronted with Jesus, he sees nothing lovely, he stands condemned. God sent Jesus in love. He sent Him for our salvation, but that which was sent in love has become condemned. It is not God who has condemned us, God only loves us, those who choose not to accept His Son, have condemned themselves. Thank You Lord for the sacrifice of Your amazing Son. Blessings

14 Good Morning!

Yea, though I walk through the valley of the shadow of death, I will fear no evil; For You are with me; Your rod and Your staff, they comfort me. **Psalms**

Because we have experienced God's divine care in the past, we are not afraid to descend into the valley of death on this day. Our God has promised to always be with us so we have His rod for protection, His staff for guidance, and His loving arms for comfort. We are so thankful and so grateful to You for being our Shepherd. Blessings

15

Good Morning!

just as the Son of Man did not come to be served, but to serve, and to give His life a ransom for many." **Matthew**

In the kingdoms of the world people compete with each other to achieve power, but in the kingdom of God true greatness comes from a humble and a willingness to serve The perfect example is Jesus himself, who during this time was about to lay down His life so that people in bondage to sin, might be set free. Sadly, when the Holy Sacrifice was preparing to go to Jerusalem to offer Himself for the sins of mankind and redeem us from the hand of Satan, the disciples did not recognize the power that Jesus possessed to save the world and Satan was doubling and redoubling his efforts to thwart God's holy purpose. We are so thankful and so grateful that things didn't work out in Satan's favor. All glory to God because we have overcome thru the power of the blood of the Lamb. Blessings

16 Good Morning!

Therefore, to him who knows to do good and does not do it, to him it is sin. **James**

Anyone who does not do the Masters' will because he does not know it, will be beaten with a few stripes, but anyone who knows the truth and does not do it, he will be beaten with many stripes. Our focus in this life is to do God's will. If we know the right way, we should live and strive to do what is right because when we don't put our knowledge into our daily practice, we are guilty of sin. Lord help us to be more obedient to Your will as we strive to please You each day. Blessings

17 Good Morning!

For God so loved the world that He gave His only begotten Son, that whoever believes in Him should not perish but have everlasting life.
John

God loved us so much that He gave His only Son as a sacrifice so that we might live. God is omniscient, He knows everything. So over 2,000 years ago, before we were a thought in our parents hearts God knew about all of our sins to come. He knew that no one else could redeem our souls. He knew that we would need a way back to Him. He gave His Son and His Son willingly died so that you and I could have everlasting life, so that we would have an opportunity to choose to live again, so that we could see Him, face to face. I'm so thankful and so grateful to God because in spite of me, He gave His Son as a ransom. He deserves our worship, our praises, and our obedience. It's an honor and a privilege to tell the world about our Lord and Savior. Tell somebody today. Blessings

18 *Good Morning!*

Therefore, whether you eat or drink, or whatever you do, do all to the glory of God. **I Corinthians**

We as Christians do wrong when we use our personal freedom in a way that causes others to sin. If by eating food that harms others, our thanksgiving for the food becomes meaningless. We should be guided in our behavior not by our knowledge of the rights we have, but by our consideration for the glory of God and the well-being of our fellows. Lord thank You for reminding us that we have a responsibility to build up, edify, strengthen, and encourage others so that You will get the glory from all that we do. Blessings

19 *Good Morning!*

took branches of palm trees and went out to meet Him, and cried out: "Hosanna! 'Blessed is He who comes in the name of the Lord!' The King of Israel!" **John**

Hosanna means save now, we pray. The spontaneity of the crowd and the palm branches suggest liberation. Jesus refuses their military and political aspirations by sitting on a donkey, symbolic of humility and peace, rather than mounting a horse, which is a symbol of conquest. The crowd's idea of Jesus's purpose was far different from His. He came to free us from sin's oppression, not from the oppression of the Romans. He is our King of King and Lord if Lords, we are grateful. Blessings

20 Good Morning!

Then He taught, saying to them, "Is it not written, 'My house shall be called a house of prayer for all nations'? But you have made it a 'den of thieves.' " **Mark**

The money changers would trade out the coins for the Jews, but they were ripping them off in the process. Jesus had already ran them away previously, but they were back trading again for exorbitant prices. All the Jews wanted to do was give God an offering, but they were dealing with people who were out for their own personal gain. Let's take an introspective look at ourselves, who or what is keeping us from giving an offering to God? Are we trading our coins for other goods and services? Are we paying all our bills before we give an offering? The scribes and chief priests sought to kill Christ and He was sinless, what are we sacrificing when we enter the church with our leftover offerings? Let's stop treating the church as common passage and begin to bring the best, our first fruits because that is holy and acceptable unto our God. Blessings

21 Good Morning!

So Jesus answered and said to them, "Assuredly, I say to you, if you have faith and do not doubt, you will not only do what was done to the fig tree, but also if you say to this mountain, 'Be removed and be cast into the sea,' it will be done. **Matthew**

Jesus's words are telling us that all who have faith in Him, are already blessed with the power to get through difficulties and any of the complications that we may face in this life. Problems that pose themselves as mountains before us will become molehills or completely flattened. Remember, when our problems threaten to become mountainous, when it seems like they are going to overtake us, don't stop, keep moving forward because just a thimble full of faith will overshadow our situation and change our perspective. Glory to God, our circumstance may not change immediately, but faith will shift our focus to the Master, He will bless us to remember the last time He brought us out, and immediately our outlook will get better. Lord thank you for reminding us of the power and blessedness of putting our faith in You. Blessings

22 Good Morning!

My brethren, count it all joy when you fall into various trials, 3 knowing that the testing of your faith produces patience. **James**

Trials are for the purpose of building courage in the believer, they are designed to bring spiritual maturity and completeness in those who believe. One of the responsibilities of being a Christian requires us to do one thing, something by nature that is very difficult, face the trials of life with joy. This joy comes through the knowledge that trials help believers to develop endurance and this in turn strengthens our Christian character. So we can count it all joy as we better understand the process and know that temptation is the testing of our faith and this testing of our faith develops patience, or works patience within us. We are so thankful for the tests and trials of life that have made us stronger and wiser in Him. Amen. Blessings

23 Good Morning!

Therefore, my beloved brethren, be steadfast, immovable, always abounding in the work of the Lord, knowing that your labor is not in vain in the Lord. **I Corinthians**

Be steadfast and settled, confide in the truth of this doctrine of the resurrection. We can't let anything shake our faith, we can't let anything move us away from the hope of the Gospel that has been give to us. We want to always abound in the work of the Lord, how can we do this? By operating in obedience to His holy word. Every believer in Christ is a workman of God. Our labor in the Lord is never in vain, we should not only work, but we need to labor or put forth all our efforts and strength in doing good by operating under His direction, and by His influence because without Him we can do absolutely nothing. Lord keep us focused on You and the work You have for us to complete. Blessings

24 Good Morning!

The fear of man brings a snare,
But whoever trusts in the Lord shall be safe.
Proverbs

   This verse draws our attention to Peter, He denied Jesus 3 times. We can understand better that the mighty have been slain, they have fallen, unless they call on the strong for strength and the courage to use it. We can't be ashamed of Jesus or His people, or His cross because He's the source of our strength. We can glory in this, because we know Him, we are joined to Him, and He counts us worthy to bear our cross and follow Him. We are grateful. Blessings

25 Good Morning!

For God has not given us a spirit of fear, but of power and of love and of a sound mind.
II Timothy

God has not given unto us the spirit of bondage, He has given us a spirit of power, to work miracles, to confuse our enemies, to support us in trials, and enable us to do what is lawful and right in His sight. He has given us a spirit of love, that enables us to hear, believe, hope, and endure all things and thus is an incentive to our obedience. He's given us a sound mind, of self-possession and government, according to some. But a sound mind implies so much more, it means a clear understanding, sound judgment, holy passions, and a heavenly temperament. It means that our entire soul is harmonized in all its powers and faculties and its completely regulated and influenced to always think, speak, and act correctly in all things. God has given us the spirit of these things, they are real, radical, powers and tempers that are produced by their proper principle that begins and ends in Christ Jesus. We are grateful. Blessings

26 Good Morning!

The thief does not come except to steal, and to kill, and to destroy. I have come that they may have life, and that they may have it more abundantly. **John**

Those who are set on stealing, killing, and destroying come into the priesthood so they can enjoy the revenues of the Church, they are the basest and vilest of thieves and murderers. Their ungodly conduct is a snare to the simple, and often the occasion of much scandal to the cause of Christ. Their doctrine is deadly and they are not commissioned by Christ, so they can't profit the people of God. How can worldly-minded, insubordinate, uncaring priests read the words of the Lord, without trembling to the center of their souls? Our God is the fountain of life. He came so that we might have an abundance of life and all good things, the blessings, the privileges, love, life, and salvation of our Lord. Even when it doesn't seem like it, we have more than enough in our Lord and Savior. Thank You Lord for blessing us to live and operate in abundance. Blessings

27 Good Morning!

And not only that, but we also glory in tribulations, knowing that tribulation produces perseverance; 4 and perseverance, character; and character, hope. 5 Now hope does not disappoint, because the love of God has been poured out in our hearts by the Holy Spirit who was given to us. **Romans**

Peace with God is nowhere more conspicuous than in the response of believers to tribulation and trial. In the place of bitterness and frustration, a disciple of Jesus will glory in difficulty simply because we know that God uses the difficulties of life to produce perseverance (endurance), character (discernment), and hope (confident assurance). We are so grateful for the Holy Spirit that has been poured into our hearts to keep us focused on your goodness. Thank you Lord. Blessings

28 Good Morning!

For the word of God is living and powerful, and sharper than any two-edged sword, piercing even to the division of soul and spirit, and of joints and marrow, and is a discerner of the thoughts and intents of the heart. **Hebrews**

The capabilities of the word of God are clearly stated here. The nature of God's word is that of life-giving communication. The word is translated as powerful, "like energy." His word is sharp and penetrating, acting like a critic or discerner of our thoughts and motivations or the purposes of our heart. Remember, the word of God has the unique ability to not only discover the level of our actions but also to reveal the hidden desires and reasonings behind our choices. Lord thank You for reminding us that all things are naked and open to You whom we must all give an account one day. We honor You Lord. Blessings

29 *Good Morning!*

praying always with all prayer and supplication in the Spirit, being watchful to this end with all perseverance and supplication for all the saints. **Ephesians 6:18 NKJV**

Prayer expresses needs that we are unable to satisfy. It is an acknowledgment that we live in total dependence on the Lord. The essence of our prayers is an admission of total helplessness combined with absolute confidence in our Savior to supply all of our need according to His riches in glory. When we live in an attitude and posture of prayer, and pray without ceasing, we are maintaining the ongoing and constant attitude of simple, childlike trust and helpless dependence on our Father. Lord we worship and praise You for an attitude and consistent posture of prayer. Blessings

30 Good Morning!

Go therefore and make disciples of all the nations, baptizing them in the name of the Father and of the Son and of the Holy Spirit. **Matthew 28:19 NKJV**

This commission from Jesus was to the whole church in every age. The baptizing and teaching ministries have the force of this mandate because they logically follow the imperative "make disciples." Matthew concludes his gospel with the blessed promise of our Lord's presence as we do our best to carry the gospel to all people. Acts 1:8 informs us that it is by the precious Holy Spirit that we are empowered for this global task. The presence of our Savior and the power of the Holy Spirit are God's twin certainties that we are to hold on to as we strive to continually and consistently serve our Lord and Savior until His return. Father, we thank you for the baptism and a spirit of obedience to follow Your command to spread the gospel to all who will hear. We are grateful. Blessings

31 Good Morning!

Your word I have hidden in my heart,
That I might not sin against You. **Psalms**

All believers should safeguard the word in their hearts as if it is a precious object that needs to be protected and treasured. We need the word in our heart so that we will be strong during the dark hours of temptation and lack of discipline. One of the keys to remaining faithful to God is to consistently speak to God about all things. Lord thank You for blessing us to understand that the strength and foundation of our obedience is a direct result of us having the word buried deep within our heart. We are grateful. Blessings

32 Good Morning!

If any of you lacks wisdom, let him ask of God, who gives to all liberally and without reproach, and it will be given to him. **James**

God gives wisdom generously. He's not stingy when He provides insight to those who ask for guidance on how to make the best choices. God gives wisdom away without "reproach" or finding fault. In other words, He doesn't look at any of our previous foolish choices and decide that we are not worthy of receiving divine wisdom from Him. He is forever faithful and completely generous towards us. All glory to God. Blessings

33

Good Morning!

But you shall receive power when the Holy Spirit has come upon you; and you shall be witnesses to Me in Jerusalem, and in all Judea and Samaria, and to the end of the earth." **Acts**

This scripture gives the agenda for Christians of all times. It is what all believers are commissioned to do until Jesus returns. God poured out the Holy Spirit on the church collectively, giving formal confirmation that the church was the entity chosen to spread the Good News throughout the world. The Holy Spirit is the Guide and Teacher who helps the church to implement the Great Commission. World evangelization requires the authority of Christ, the presence of Christ, the power of the Spirit, and obedient and available saints. When believers are Spirit filled, we can witness with power from on high. The Great Commission remains a very present mandate for every generation until the Lord returns. Lord we thank You for positioning us to do our part to spread the Good News. Blessings

34

Good Morning!

"Let not your heart be troubled; you believe in God, believe also in Me. 2 In My Father's house are many mansions; if it were not so, I would have told you. I go to prepare a place for you. 3 And if I go and prepare a place for you, I will come again and receive you to Myself; that where I am, there you may be also. **John**

The word for mansions can be translated resting place or permanent dwelling place. Clearly, Jesus knew that the disciples anticipated some such heavenly dwelling. He assures them that He would have corrected the notion if it were not true. The place where Christians will abide is a prepared place in heaven. It is impossible to determine heaven's location, we are promised the escort of Jesus Himself and then eternal fellowship with the Lord. "I am coming back" is an explicit statement from Christ's lips. He is coming back! His purpose will be to receive us. Thank you Lord for preparing an eternal place for us. Amen! Blessings

35

Good Morning!

And God will wipe away every tear from their eyes; there shall be no more death, nor sorrow, nor crying. There shall be no more pain, for the former things have passed away." **Revelation**

When it's all over, the Lord declares that He will wipe away every tear. Better days are coming, and God is working to bring an end to all the pain and suffering that we endure daily. As we place our trust in Him, we are assured that a new Kingdom is waiting for us, one that makes every minute of every day, regardless of what it looks like, totally worthwhile! God will wipe away our tears and there will be no more death, sorrow or pain. Lord, we honor and glorify You. Blessings

36 Good Morning!

Peace I leave with you, My peace I give to you; not as the world gives do I give to you. Let not your heart be troubled, neither let it be afraid. **John**

This is a promise of eternal peace to all believers in the midst of our troubles we can have peace. Not knowing what the outcome or end may be brings its own kind of terror. As we experience things, we are not as nervous as we were the first time we experienced it. As we experience different things our expectations change because we know what's happening and we understand what will happen next. This brings about confidence, it reduces our fear and allows us to have peace regarding the issue. The peace that Christ offers comes with hope and assurance that's greater than anything the world can offer. His peace is permanent, guaranteed, and eternal (Heb. 6:18–19). As we experience situations and circumstances that threaten us or cause fear and frustration, let's try to acknowledge the reality of the suffering that living brings while we trust in God to make good on His promise of perfect peace. Blessings

37 Good Morning!

Do you not know that you are the temple of God and that the Spirit of God dwells in you? **I Corinthians**

The temple is the unique dwelling place of the Spirit of God. Paul is asking his readers, as the local church in Corinth, if they understand that they together are God's temple and that God's Spirit lives in them. So, we are God's temple. If anyone attempts to destroy God's people, in any manner, the promise of God is that He will destroy that person. Don't ever be afraid to let others know who you belong to. Thank you Lord. Blessings

38

Good Morning!

For I am persuaded that neither death nor life, nor angels nor principalities nor powers, nor things present nor things to come, 39 nor height nor depth, nor any other created thing, shall be able to separate us from the love of God which is in Christ Jesus our Lord. **Romans**

God is for us, God will freely give us all things, He has justified us, He prays for us, and we cannot be separated from His love. All of these precious blessings are granted to those of us who are in Christ. With encouragements like these, the Christian can endure suffering with hope and assurance. Our Master has embraced us in such an absolute way, that nothing can get between us and God's love. We are forever grateful. Blessings

39

Good Morning!

Therefore, as the elect of God, holy and beloved, put on tender mercies, kindness, humility, meekness, longsuffering;
Colossians

As the chosen ones, the sanctified ones, the holy children of God, we should be disciplined and we ought to show compassion, kindness, humility, gentleness and patience towards others. We are to strive to be holy because He is holy. As the elect of God, we are the representatives of Christ. Thank you Lord for choosing us. We are grateful. Blessings

40

Good Morning!

However, when He, the Spirit of truth, has come, He will guide you into all truth; for He will not speak on His own authority, but whatever He hears He will speak; and He will tell you things to come. **John 16:13 NKJV**

The Spirit will guide us into the truth that is useful to men and profitable to churches. He is our guide, He goes before us, removes obstructions, opens our understanding, and makes all things plain for us. Lord we thank you for the guidance and eternal direction of Your Spirit. We are so thankful and so grateful for your loving kindness. Blessings

41 Good Morning!

Whenever I am afraid, I will trust in You.
Psalms

We must remember, during any test or trial we can recite Psalm 56:3 for our resolve, to center us, and to help us to focus. Anytime we are afraid, we can trust in the Lord. This scripture teaches us, when we are scared of what people will do to us or say to us we should strengthen ourselves in God. There are times when we will be terrified because of what may be happening to us, because the difficulties of life will find us, but never forget, we have an anchor in our Lord and Savior, Jesus Christ. Thank you Lord for teaching us not to fear, but to put our trust in You. Blessings

42

Good Morning!

And be kind to one another, tenderhearted, forgiving one another, even as God in Christ forgave you. **Ephesians**

We need to consistently strive to be kind, compassionate, and forgiving towards one another. Forgiveness is a matter that is dear to God's heart because forgiveness paid a tremendous part in the redemption of mankind. Forgiveness of sin is what sinful people desire, but they remain incapable of receiving it unless they come to the foot of the Cross and accept the cleansing blood of the Lamb because there is no forgiveness of sin except through the shed blood of our Lord and Savior Jesus Christ. Lord, thank you for our Savior and Waymaker We are grateful. Blessings

43

Good Morning!

Keep your heart with all diligence, For out of it spring the issues of life. **Proverbs**

The command center of our soul is our heart and it controls the mind, will, and affections of every believer. What is hidden in the heart is open to God's eyes. So, it is absolutely essential that we guard our heart daily. Our heart is very influential in how we live out our morals and values. Lord thank you for blessing us with as heart that produces good so that You can get the glory from all we do. We are grateful. Blessings

44

Good Morning!

If we confess our sins, He is faithful and just to forgive us our sins and to cleanse us from all unrighteousness. **I John**

Characteristic of authentic Christianity is the confession of sin. Confession includes both an acknowledgment of a specific sin and the recognition that sin needs to be forgiven. In response to confession, God is faithful and just. He is faithful by honoring His promises to forgive sin (Jeramiah. 31:34). He is just because the death of His Son provides us with the moral ground for divine forgiveness. When we have an argument or disagreement with others, it creates a barrier to fellowship. Since a barrier between us and God will always be our fault, our need for confession is important for our relationship with God, the only One who can cleanse us from all unrighteousness, to prosper spiritually. All glory to God. Blessings

45

Good Morning!

bearing with one another, and forgiving one another, if anyone has a complaint against another; even as Christ forgave you, so you also must do. **Colossians**

Forgiveness involves completely letting go of any resentment or faults toward others. Christians are family so we should quickly extend kindness and grace to one another. This includes being able to forgive, as well as tolerating the different peculiarities or oddities of others. Let's strive to operate in forgiveness without holding grudges or bringing the issue up as a reminder to hurt others. God doesn't remind us of things that He has forgiven us for.. Lord we thank You. Blessings

46

Good Morning!

There is therefore now no condemnation to those who are in Christ Jesus, who do not walk according to the flesh, but according to the Spirit. **Romans**

One of the most powerful and most gracious of God's promises is written in this verse. We have the word condemnation that can be translated judgment. So in this verse we learn that there is no judgment for those of us who are in Christ because sin has already been judged in the substitutionary atonement of our Lord and Savior, Jesus Christ. Lord, we thank You for blessing us to know and understand that salvation is for those of us who place our faith in your Son, Jesus (Romans 3:23–26). There is absolutely, no other way (Acts 4:12), so those who reject this salvation will most definitely not be rescued from judgement. We offer You all the praise Lord because only You are worthy. Blessings

47

Good Morning!

But as many as received Him, to them He gave the right to become children of God, to those who believe in His name: **John**

Many in His own home town rejected Him. This is so sad. They will be condemned for their rejection, not their ignorance. God gave the grace so people would accept the gift. As believers, we become children, partakers of the divine nature. To believe in the name means to accept who and what the Person is. Being a child of God does not come about by human or physical descent, nor is it attributed to human volition or the action of men. It is a sovereign work of God that provides for and accomplishes our salvation. Lord we are thankful. Blessings

48 Good Morning!

Teach me to do Your will, For You are my God; Your Spirit is good. Lead me in the land of uprightness. **Psalms**

There are no greater words that God desires to hear from us than these "teach me to do your will." This is what it means for Him to be God, to have complete control over our lives and for Him to be the head of our thought processes in every situation. Giving God this kind of control over us or just putting forth the effort to put Him first is a key factor of loving God with all of our heart, soul, mind, and strength. Lord thank You for giving us an opportunity to love You with all that's within us. We are grateful. Blessings

49 *Good Morning!*

Strength and honor are her clothing;
She shall rejoice in time to come.
26 She opens her mouth with wisdom,
And on her tongue is the law of kindness.
Proverbs

When we take a look around at our world today, we often find that some of our women and Mothers are lacking in virtue or a moral standard. A virtuous woman depends on God, not her boo or her sugar daddy.. Because this virtuous woman seeks God in all her ways, she is not afraid of her future or anxious about anything that comes her way. Her future is bright because God is a strong presence in her life so she can rejoice at the days ahead because she has a relationship with God and she continually seeks Him first. We have heard the saying, behind every great man there is a great woman. We are tweaking that a little today.. Behind every great man there is a great woman, and it is not his wife, it is his mother. No woman has the influence, the opportunity, the privilege, or the reward of a mother. A mother's love and training does more to cultivate, transform, and mold character for life than ten wives. This mother treats her children with kindness, kindness indicates that she is able and willing to give moral and spiritual instruction to her children. They listen because when she speaks, her words are wise, and her tone and demeanor are affectionate and gentle. Thank God for our nurturing and attentive Mothers. Blessings

50 *Good Morning!*

that the God of our Lord Jesus Christ, the Father of glory, may give to you the spirit of wisdom and revelation in the knowledge of Him, **Ephesians**

Paul is specific with who He is praying to, God the Father. We need to be just as specific with our own prayers. This verse expresses a prayer request for spiritual enlightenment concerning our salvation and our Savior. Thank you Lord for making the simple things in life plain by teaching us to stay connected to you through our prayer life so that we may be positioned appropriately to receive all that You have promised us and that we may be familiar with the plan that You have predestined and preordained for our lives. We are humbly grateful. Blessings

51 Good Morning!

And the Word became flesh and dwelt among us, and we beheld His glory, the glory as of the only begotten of the Father, full of grace and truth. **John**

It's probably the heresy that Jesus seemed to be human is what John is combatting here. John insists that Christ is really human: He was tired and thirsty (4:6-7), He wept (11-35), He was troubled in his spirit (12:27, 13:21), and He died (19:30). He did all those things without becoming less than God (Phil. (2:5-11), Jesus took upon Himself complete human nature. At His carnation, God became God-Man. He dwelt among us. So John could speak of hearing, seeing, and touching Him. We are so thankful that the bright cloud of God's glorious Person settled upon the tabernacle, Exodus (24:16), (40:35), so in Christ, God's glorious Person still dwells among us. Let's magnify the Lord on this day for our Comforter, the Holy Spirit. Blessings

52 *Good Morning!*

Therefore whoever hears these sayings of Mine, and does them, I will liken him to a wise man who built his house on the rock.
Matthew

The wise man will build his house upon the rock of Jesus's words. The foolish man will build his house on the frivolous sands of the world. From the Day of Judgment onward, the thing that will distinguish wise men from the foolish is their reward. The wise man's rewards are determined by whether he acts or does not act on the words and promises of Jesus Christ, our Lord and Savior. We must strive to be doers of the word so that all that we accomplish will be pleasing in the sight of God, our walk will be bold and purposeful, and the kingdom of heaven will be available to us when it's time. Lord we are grateful. Blessings

53

Good Morning!

One thing I have desired of the Lord, That will I seek: That I may dwell in the house of the Lord All the days of my life, To behold the beauty of the Lord, And to inquire in His temple. **Psalms**

David's top priority in life was perfecting his relationship with the Lord. Even though he was in the wilderness looking for refuge from his enemies, his heart was in the tabernacle seeking the beauty of God. When he was in the wilderness running for his life, David's desire was to return to the tabernacle and spend the rest of his life in worship and fellowship with the Lord continually seeking God's presence and His favor. Lord we thank you for the example of David, bless us Lord with a desire to seek You and Your presence as eagerly and boldly as David did. We honor and adore You. Blessings

54 Good Morning!

I have been crucified with Christ; it is no longer I who live, but Christ lives in me; and the life which I now live in the flesh I live by faith in the Son of God, who loved me and gave Himself for me. **Galatians**

We have been taught that the Old Testament is the book of the Law. The law functions to declare our guilt, drive us to Christ, and to give us direction in living a life of obedience, but the law is powerless to save our souls. In this scripture Paul is explaining to us how he has been crucified with Christ and is now positionally dead to the Mosaic Law (Romans 7:6). His life, just as our lives are, is no longer a self-effort in keeping the law, it is a life empowered by the indwelling Spirit of Christ. Thank You Lord for grace. If we try to compare the functions of Law and Grace, Romans helps us to understand..the law is based on works (3:10), grace is based on faith (3: 11,12), the law is our guardian (4:2), grace is centered in Christ (3:24), the law is our tutor (3:24), grace is our certificate of freedom (4:30, 31). Lord we are grateful for the provision of the perfect standard of the Law so that we can measure ourselves morally and spiritually. Thank you for allowing us to see our imperfections so we can come to Christ in faith for deliverance and salvation. In humble obedience and great gratitude we come to You on this day abundantly thankful for grace. Blessings

55

Good Morning!

I will both lie down in peace, and sleep; For You alone, O Lord, make me dwell in safety.
Psalms

With God on our side we can lie down in peace. Even during our dark moments and difficult situations, our sleep can be pleasant and refreshing. We can sleep and rest safely because God is our peace and our lives are in His capable hands. Many individuals lie down, but they can't sleep because of their anxieties and their inability to slow their thought processes when it's time to rest. Lord we thank you for calmness and serenity of our mind, in the midst of all the troubles of our lives. We are grateful to have the opportunity to swell in yourself safety daily. Blessings

56 *Good Morning!*

For all the law is fulfilled in one word, even in this: "You shall love your neighbor as yourself." **Galatians**

As we bear one another's burdens, we are fulfilling the Law. When we serve in love, everything else falls into place. We can't serve the law because it was fulfilled in Christ. Love is the essence of all of God's law. Remember, people who pray for one another rarely prey on one another. Thank you Lord for reminding us that we are free, that Jesus has fully paid for all of our sins, that we are completely justified before God by being in Christ, and that we need to love our neighbor as ourselves daily. We are grateful. Blessings

57

Good Morning!

O Lord, You are my God. I will exalt You, I will praise Your name, For You have done wonderful things; Your counsels of old are faithfulness and truth. **Isaiah**

God has always had a remnant of believers who trust His Word, believe His promises, and who will drop everything to give glory to His holy name even when the experiences of this life and the ungodly behaviors of others seem to indicate the opposite. We must remember, regardless of the tests and trials that we encounter each day, we will always be a part of the remnant of believers who trust God, believe in His promises, glorify His name, and honor Him with praise. Lord, we are grateful. Blessings

58 Good Morning!

Therefore comfort each other and edify one another, just as you also are doing.
I Thessalonians

Encouraging and inspiring others is an important part of loving them just like we love ourselves. Providing encouragement and inspiration is extremely important for Christians because most of the people whom God allows to cross our path are hurting in some form or fashion. As we encourage others, we lift them up, support them, and reassure them by offering them hope. Let's strive to be more compassionate and sensitive members of the kingdom because it's easier to inspire someone who feels encouraged just like it's easier to encourage someone who feels inspired. Thank you Lord for teaching us how to comfort one another. Blessings

59 *Good Morning!*

Continue earnestly in prayer, being vigilant in it with thanksgiving; **Colossians**

Being watchful and alert over our soul and attuned to spiritual things is not a cause for us to doubt our standing with Christ, it's actually a sign of wisdom because we live in a world of trials, difficult tests, and dangers to our soul. This is a reminder to us for the need for us to pray continuously and vigorously in a posture of thanksgiving because we are completely dependent on our God to be all that we need Him to be each and every day of our lives. Thank You Lord for always being a present help for us. We are grateful. Blessings

60 *Good Morning!*

casting all your care upon Him, for He cares for you. **I Peter**

This scripture gives words of encouragement to all of us who are overwhelmed with the burdens and challenges of this life. Peter is telling us to take our anxieties and worries and present them to our God, the One who truly cares for us. As soon as we lay our worries and issues before Him, they are no longer our responsibility. Thank You Lord for promising to carry our burdens, cares, and issues. We are trusting You to handle them so that all things will work out for our good. You alone are worthy Lord. Blessings

61 Good Morning!

For the poor you have with you always, but Me you do not have always." **John**

Mary thought that this would be the last time she saw Jesus so she washed his feet with her hair. Jesus saw this act as a symbolic anointing of his body in preparation for his burial. Judas objected to her cleaning Jesus' feet with the expensive perfume because he felt that the gesture was trivial and wasteful. Jesus explained to him that this was a symbolic anointing of his body in preparation for burial. The priority of Jesus and ensuring that His requirements and standards are upheld take precedence over the legitimate needs of the poor. As we strive for greater in Him remember, the fulfillment of the basic needs of the poor and all else is secondary to the completion of the will of our Lord and Savior. We are humbled. Blessings

62

Good Morning!

19 And He took bread, gave thanks and broke it, and gave it to them, saying, "This is My body which is given for you; do this in remembrance of Me." 20 Likewise He also took the cup after supper, saying, "This cup is the new covenant in My blood, which is shed for you. **Luke**

The disciples knew that Jesus spoke metaphorically of the bread as His body and the fruit of the vine as His blood. The supper would serve as a memorial that God Himself secured man's redemption, through the suffering of the incarnate Christ (the bread) and the shedding of His blood (the cup), in vicarious (secondhand) atonement. This is the new covenant because it is a covenant of grace and forgiveness based on the shed blood of Jesus. Lord we thank You for the new covenant, thank You for putting the law in our minds and writing Your word in our hearts, thank You for being our God and for allowing us to be Your people. Thank You for being available so that we can all have an opportunity to know You, thank You for forgiving our iniquities and our sins, and we glorify You Lord for never remembering any of them once You forgive us. And Lord, we thank You for the blood of Your Son that sealed this covenant so that we may experience this unconditional promise of forgiveness and eternal life that is available to all who will receive Jesus Christ as Lord and Savior of our lives. Blessings

63

Good Morning!

But He was wounded for our transgressions, He was bruised for our iniquities; The chastisement for our peace was upon Him, And by His stripes we are healed. **Isaiah**

The substitutionary nature of His suffering and death, in which Jesus laid down His own life on behalf of every man who would accept His redemption, is set forth. The punishment of our sins was inflicted on Him so our peace and reconciliation with God was made by Him. Sin is a disease belonging to all men, a natural, hereditary, nauseous, and incurable one, but by the blood of Christ, forgiving sin is a healing of this disease. When we obey, our sins will be forgiven, but forgiveness is not through our obedience, it's through the blood of Christ. We are so thankful and so grateful for the shedding of the blood of our Lord and Savior. Blessings

64

Good Morning!

Therefore my heart is glad, and my glory rejoices; My flesh also will rest in hope. 10 For You will not leave my soul in Sheol, Nor will You allow Your Holy One to see corruption. **Psalms**

Our hearts are totally glad in God, always full of the Divine presence because whatever we do pleases Him. Our tongue rejoiced because it was bestowed on us to glorify Him and because it is our glory, it's the instrument of expressing our thoughts by words. Jesus, as He hung on the cross and breathed out His soul with His life, saw that His rest in the grave would be very short, just a sufficiency of time to prove the reality of His death, but not long enough to produce corruption. Just like His soul wasn't in the grave long enough to produce corruption in the darkness of Sheol neither will ours be, those of us who have accepted Him as our Lord and Savior. Thank You Lord for pouring out your Spirit that we see and hear daily. Blessings

65 Good Morning!

But he said to them, "Do not be alarmed. You seek Jesus of Nazareth, who was crucified. He is risen! He is not here. See the place where they laid Him. **Mark**

The Messiah did indeed come to suffer and die for the sins of His people, but His death did not mean defeat. He was vindicated and victorious through His resurrection. The resurrection also provided the possibility of His return "with great power and glory", when He will establish the kingdom the Jews anticipated. The resurrection of Jesus Christ is significant for the believer because His resurrection is the guarantee of our own resurrection and glorification. Jesus was crucified in our place so that we would not need to receive God's curse over us, but may instead receive His blessings. We are so thankful and so grateful to Him for giving His life for us. Blessings

66 Good Morning!

I am the good shepherd. The good shepherd gives His life for the sheep. **John**

Jesus is the Good Shepherd. He places Himself in contrast to Israel's religious leaders, who were supposed to be faithful shepherds, but were more like those evil false shepherds described in Ezekiel 34. He is also "the door of the sheep" not the fold. Jesus is in charge of and cares for the lives of the sheep. To emphasize the access to God He provides, He calls Himself "the door" apart from whom no one enters the fold. Thank You Jesus for laying down Your life for us. We are grateful. Blessings

67

Good Morning!

And Jesus said to them, "I am the bread of life. He who comes to Me shall never hunger, and he who believes in Me shall never thirst. **John**

He is the bread that gives life and preserves us from death. All who will receive His doctrine and believe in Him as the great atoning sacrifice will be perfectly satisfied and free from having a miserable mind. All the guilt of our sins will be blotted out and our souls will be purified unto God and we will be able to love Him with all our heart, we will rest fully, supremely, and finally happy, in our God. This bread from heaven is a spiritual provision available to those who being drawn by the Father to the Son, give themselves to Him in faith. We are grateful. Blessings

68

Good Morning!

Then Jesus spoke to them again, saying, "I am the light of the world. He who follows Me shall not walk in darkness, but have the light of life." **John**

At the Court of the Women in the temple, a golden lampstand was lighted during the Feast of the tabernacles. Again Jesus utilizes a convenient symbol for Himself that is rooted in the Old Testament, imagery of the wanderings in the wilderness. In ch. 6, it was the manna, in ch. 7 it was the water associated with God's provision from the rock. Now, the lighting of the giant lamps reminded the nation of the pillar of fire which guided them at night. In contrast to the moral darkness of the nation and the world in general, Jesus describes His function as the Light, the very revelation and truth of God, and the solution to the evil in mankind and the world. Thank You Lord for the Light of Jesus our solution to the evil in this world. We are grateful. Blessings

69 Good Morning!

Abide in Me, and I in you. As the branch cannot bear fruit of itself, unless it abides in the vine, neither can you, unless you abide in Me. 5 "I am the vine, you are the branches. He who abides in Me, and I in him, bears much fruit; for without Me you can do nothing. **John**

Jesus is the vinedresser. His purpose in our life is not to judge but to produce fruit, thereby rendering aid to a faltering vine. He also continually cleanses us in order to maximize the fruit. To be without fruit means that Jesus' goal for our life has been frustrated. It signifies either a false follower or a useless disciple such as Judas. False followers or the fruitless ones only benefit is to provide fuel for fire. The presence of false disciples in the church is not an unusual phenomenon, they are present, but they have no spiritual union with Him. We must strive to abide in Christ, abiding in Him sets us up to be fruitful, it is also the beginning of effectual prayer, consistent obedience, purposeful joy, and an abundance of peace. Lord, help us to be fruitful effective branches on the vines of this life. Blessings

70

Good Morning!

Jesus said to him, "I am the way, the truth, and the life. No one comes to the Father except through Me. **John**

Jesus doesn't simply show the way, He is the Way. He doesn't simply reveal the truth, He is the truth. He doesn't simply give life, He is the life. All the concepts and abstractions are turned into a person. The way the truth and the life describe the three principle aspects of the Exodus. The Way out of bondage, the truth which guides us in living the Christian life, and the power to live a life pleasing to Christ. In the Person of Christ, we not only have the statement but we have the fact of moral perfection realized. John plainly teaches that life is found in the Person of Jesus Christ. All who have Jesus Christ have life. All who choose to live without Him have no life. We are grateful to have a path to the Father through our Lord and Savior Jesus Christ. Blessings

71

Good Morning!

But may the God of all grace, who called us to His eternal glory by Christ Jesus, after you have suffered a while, perfect, establish, strengthen, and settle you.
I Peter

God never promised that we would not experience hardships, tests, and trials. In His kindness, God called us to share in His eternal glory by means of Christ. So before, after and during, our trials and tribulations that He has called us to, He will restore us, support us, strengthen us, and position us to be able to stand on a firm foundation that is based on His Son, Jesus, so while we still have time let's plug in, turn on and prepare to be settled in His will. All glory to God! Blessings

72 Good Morning!

For "whoever calls on the name of the Lord shall be saved." **Romans**

There are no distinctions in our Lord and Savior. Everyone has the same opportunity to be saved. So whoever calls on Him will most definitely be saved. As we believe in our heart, we are made righteous before God. When we state our belief through our own mouth our salvation is confirmed in the heavens. Lord, thank you for keeping salvation simple for us, all we need to do is call on You, believe in You, and confess our faults and You will move on our behalf and save us. Blessings

73 *Good Morning!*

Do not be wise in your own eyes;
Fear the Lord and depart from evil.
Proverbs

Never let yourself think that you are wiser than you are, just strive to obey the Lord and refuse to do wrong. God is calling us to complete commitment so that we can experience the happiness and blessing of trusting in Him. Remember, true wisdom is only found in the Lord and in His holy word. Thank You Lord for reminding us that our confidence and trust should be rooted and grounded in You. We can better understand, as our trust grows deeper in You, our confidence will increase exponentially. We are grateful. Blessings

74 Good Morning!

bears all things, believes all things, hopes all things, endures all things.
I Corinthians

The Corinthians were impressed with people who exercised the more spectacular gifts. Paul reminds them that no matter what gifts they have tongues, prophecy, wisdom, knowledge, or faith, if they lack love they are not just unimportant, they are nothing. Thank You Lord for love that upholds Your standard of righteousness, love that always rejoices in what is true, and never in what is wrong. Thank You for a love that is trusting and persevering, and always looks positively to the ultimate fulfillment of Your purposes. We are so thankful and so grateful to have Your love in our hearts. Blessings

75 Good Morning!

Beloved, do not imitate what is evil, but what is good. He who does good is of God, but he who does evil has not seen God. **III John**

Do not imitate the wicked. Our conduct should be merciful loving and kind. Whoever does good is of God and he will enjoy the divine appropriation of God. Whoever does evil by being unmerciful, unfeeling and unkind will have no proper knowledge of God whose name is mercy and whose nature is love. Lord please help us to strive to do good and to show loving kindness to all daily. Blessings

76

Good Morning!

13 For You formed my inward parts;
You covered me in my mother's womb.
14 I will praise You, for I am fearfully and wonderfully made; Marvelous are Your works, And that my soul knows very well.
Psalms

This passage extols God for His marvelous work in human creation and constitutes the most important pericope in scripture on one's self-image. God prescribed the custom design for each individual to equip us for specific achievement and purpose. The creator never finishes but continues to edify and build up the creation because as the creator He receives glory or dishonor according to the fruits of His creation. We can achieve a wholesome self-image by recognizing the lordship of the Creator in our life through a continuous and systematic quiet time of reading the word and praying, through a careful assessment of our priorities, and by building a personal image according to God's blueprint. God does not assess personal worth as man does, He looks beyond our bodily frame to the picture within. Blessings

77 Good Morning!

You are of God, little children, and have overcome them, because He who is in you is greater than he who is in the world. **I John**

Greater is He that is within me than he that is in the world. Thank God for the Holy Spirit who lives in us. We have overcome by the blood of the Lamb and we are grateful. God cares for those of us who trust in Him, this will assure us the victory over the enemy because He lives on the inside of us. All glory to God. Blessings

78 Good Morning!

As iron sharpens iron, So a man sharpens the countenance of his friend. **Proverbs**

Where there is true understanding, differences of personality and viewpoints can be a benefit to all concerned. Faithfulness to one another brings its reward. Thank you Lord for blessing us to understand, while one iron implement is sharpened by another an individual can sharpen the perception of their companion. Two minds acting on one accord with each other can actually become more settled and acute for all involved. Blessings

79 Good Morning!

Now faith is the substance of things hoped for, the evidence of things not seen.
Hebrews

Faith means we are certain of the things we hope for and convinced of the things we do not see. It was because of faith that the men of old time had their record verified. It is by faith that we understand that the world was fashioned by the word of our God, meaning what is seen came into existence out of what is unseen. The things hoped for are the peace and approval of God, the new heavens and the new earth. The things unseen are the creation of the world from nothing, the miraculous conception of Christ, His resurrection from the dead, and His ascension to glory. We firmly believe all of these on the testimony of God's word as if we had seen them. We are grateful for our "now faith" in every sense of the word. Thank you Lord. Blessings

80

Good Morning!

that there should be no schism in the body, but that the members should have the same care for one another. 26 And if one member suffers, all the members suffer with it; or if one member is honored, all the members rejoice with it. 27 Now you are the body of Christ, and members individually. **I Corinthians**

God never intended for us to have division in the church so He is reminding us that we need to always stay together and support one another because we represent the body of Christ individually and collectively. Thank you Lord for allowing us the opportunity to represent the body as a whole and ourselves individually, we are grateful. Blessings

81 Good Morning!

For if you remain completely silent at this time, relief and deliverance will arise for the Jews from another place, but you and your father's house will perish. Yet who knows whether you have come to the kingdom for such a time as this?" **Esther**

Esther risked her life by agreeing to go before the king, but before she went, she asked all the Jews to fast for 3 days on her behalf. Mordecai believed that God had positioned Esther for such a time as this. How many of us has God positioned for greater? How many of us know deep within our heart that God has prepared us for a greater purpose than the one we are fulfilling now? Even though God chooses to use us, He is by no means dependent on us. Let's seek His face, put our excuses aside, and get locked in and engaged with the plan of our Lord and Savior because we don't know who will be delivered and set free because we chose to be obedient to His will just like Esther. Surrender your will and He will fill the empty spaces in your life. Blessings

82

Good Morning!

Charm is deceitful and beauty is passing, But a woman who fears the Lord, she shall be praised. **Proverbs**

Charm and beauty are defined by human convention so they are transitory. A woman who fears the Lord has success and praise that comes from her godly character rather than from external and temporary devices. She elicits blessings from her children, devotion from her husband, praise from the beneficent labors of her own hands, and commendation from God Himself. She possesses the fear of the Lord, that foundation of all wisdom and the principle occupying the heart of the entire Book of Proverbs. Thank you Lord for women who possess these good qualities, thank you for women who are guided and governed by principles of conscience and a positive regard to our God. We are grateful. Blessings

83

Good Morning!

He who is faithful in what is least is faithful also in much; and he who is unjust in what is least is unjust also in much. **Luke**

We are taught to be wise stewards of this world's goods so that we can enter the kingdom of heaven. Jesus contrasts faithfulness to unfaithfulness regarding the world's goods. Jesus describes these goods as least in importance, while God's riches are described as the most important. The world's goods are described as unrighteous mammon, another man's God's. In contrast heaven's riches are much and true, riches that are our own. Being faithful with what God has entrusted us with in the earth is small when compared to what God will entrust us with in eternity regarding spiritual riches. While the world measures success by the amount of financial gain. God measures success by a person's degree of faithfulness. Lord we need you to increase our faithfulness so that we will be better stewards over all that You have entrusted to us. Thank you Lord. Blessings

84

Good Morning!

rejoicing in hope, patient in tribulation, continuing steadfastly in prayer. **Romans**

Other people are always watching us so as we are called to go through we need to rejoice in the hope that should be a constant in our lives, we need to be patient with the process within the test because we are called and equipped to maintain a focused and diligent prayer life. Our success lies within our obedience to His will, thank You Lord for being our guide. Blessings

85 Good Morning!

Set your mind on things above, not on things on the earth. **Colossians**

We waste so much time focusing on what we can accumulate in the natural that we often forget to seek those spiritual things that will sustain us not only in this life but in eternity. Many of us are falling short when it comes to sending up prayers for the generations that are coming behind us. Because we have died to sin, we are not in bondage to the things of this world. We have been raised with Christ to new life in a higher world where our desires and conduct are like Christ. Let's strive to have thoughts and actions that will allow us to lay up treasures in heaven, to concern ourselves with things that will settle us and prepare us for greater, and increase our desire to be with Christ, where He dwells, where our final home will be, where our greatest interests rest, with our Lord and Savior. We are grateful. Blessings

86 Good Morning!

Be still, and know that I am God; I will be exalted among the nations, I will be exalted in the earth! **Psalms**

We need to stop murmuring and complaining when we are called to a season of tough times so that we can reflect on God's severity and His goodness. As we go through, we must remind ourselves that He is the fountain of power, justice, wisdom, goodness, and truth. As we experience His punishments, we will know Him to be just, as we study His word, we will learn of His goodness. As we endure our hardships, we will allow Him to get the glory and proclaim salvation in every nation, among every people, and in every tongue. Be encouraged family because no matter what troubles we meet as we continue to wholeheartedly trust in God, our troubles, issues, and unusual circumstances will not overtake us. Lord thank You for Your power that smashes all opposition, thank You for being our supreme God, than You for being the supreme ruler of world. We are grateful. Blessings

87 Good Morning!

Does not rejoice in iniquity, but rejoices in the truth. **I Corinthians**

Love is one of the dynamic terms Paul uses to speak of the holy life enabled by the fullness of the Holy Spirit. It encompasses motive and deed. Love is characteristic of the mature believer. Love is not envious of evil doers and love would never rejoice in the iniquity of those who do evil. Love gladly turns its back on those who despise her and prays for them but she would never rejoice in their iniquity. Love rejoices only in the truth and in true. All that is a lie or a deception is a sorrow to love. Thank you Lord for allowing us to experience a love that believes your promises, believes the good tidings of grace, believes the power of the Gospel to save to the utmost because it believes all things. We are grateful. Blessings

88

Good Morning!

You shall love the Lord your God with all your heart, with all your soul, and with all your strength. **Deuteronomy**

Who can boast that the one absorbing object of his heart and soul is God? Or enjoy that His strength is devoted to God's pleasure? This law is a perfectly righteous one, but man in the flesh is totally incapable of obeying it. The Lord Jesus is the only one who has done so. This scripture expresses the highest truth of God's unity and uniqueness and it shows us the absolute duty of loving Him with every faculty of our being. Thank you Lord for the heart, soul, and strength of Your love. Blessings

89

Good Morning!

Seek the Lord while He may be found, Call upon Him while He is near. 7 Let the wicked forsake his way, And the unrighteous man his thoughts; Let him return to the Lord, And He will have mercy on him; And to our God, For He will abundantly pardon. **Isaiah**

We need to turn from our wicked ways, get the word deep within us so that even our thoughts will be cleansed so that we will obtain mercy from our Lord and Savior and He will have an opportunity to position us to receive more compassion, more forgiveness, and an abundance of love as we seek more of Him. We are so thankful and so grateful that He is still available to us. Blessings

90

Good Morning!

looking unto Jesus, the author and finisher of our faith, who for the joy that was set before Him endured the cross, despising the shame, and has sat down at the right hand of the throne of God. **Hebrews**

We should place all our hope and confidence in Christ because He is our sole helper in this race of faith. Our desire is for all all men to consider Him their leader in this contest and to imitate His example. So, let's have eyes only for Jesus who is the author and finisher of our faith. We may glance at other saints as they run this race, but we must gaze upon our Savior, the One who is waiting at the finish line. Above the great cloud of witnesses is the great King himself, Jesus our Lord and Savior. Some may doubt His ability to bless us to prevail against our trials, there should be no doubt about this for those of us who believe. Remember, He does see, know, understand, and eternally intercede on our behalf that we might indeed win the ultimate prize, seeing Him. Thank you Lord. Blessings

91 *Good Morning!*

Do not be overcome by evil, but overcome evil with good. **Romans**

Do not, by giving place to evil, become precisely the same character whom you condemned in someone else. Overcome evil with good, however often he grieves your spirit and compound your emotions, always repay him with kindness. Your good will and positive attitude will overcome his evil, repay his curses with blessings, and cover his misery with calmness and the love of God. The strength and power of the Lord that lies within you has already overcome the evil that others are burdened and weighed down with when they come to tear you down. Stand tall, you've already won because He created you to be an overcomer. Blessings

92

Good Morning!

In Him we have redemption through His blood, the forgiveness of sins, according to the riches of His grace. **Ephesians**

God has glorified His grace by giving us redemption by the blood of His Son, and this redemption persists in forgiving and delivering us from our sins so then Christ's blood was the redemption price that was paid down for our salvation and this was according to the riches of His grace. His abundant grace is manifested in beneficence to mankind, in our redemption by the sacrifice of Christ since the measure of redeeming grace is the measure of God's own eternal goodness. Lord we are grateful for the redemptive power of the blood. Blessings

93

Good Morning!

He who dwells in the secret place of the Most High Shall abide under the shadow of the Almighty. 2 I will say of the Lord, "He is my refuge and my fortress; My God, in Him I will trust." **Psalms**

All who legitimately enter into the secret place, the holiest of holies are guaranteed to be covered with the cloud of God's glory and the protection of our all-sufficient God. This was the privilege of the high priest only, under the law, but under the new covenant all believers in Christ have boldness to enter into the holiest by the blood of Jesus and anyone who trust to enter in are safe from every evil. Not some evil but every evil that may come against us, we have the victory because we can enjoy the security and protection of trusting in God and living our lives constantly in His presence. Thank you Lord for creating an unhindered path to the holiest of holies so that we can experience Your presence at all times. Blessings

94 Good Morning!

being confident of this very thing, that He who has begun a good work in you will complete it until the day of Jesus Christ;
Philippians

The day of Jesus Christ is a reference to the return of Christ. Paul's confidence concerning the Philippians' ability to remain in a state of salvation until that day is not based on his estimate of them, which was high, but their salvation was based on the power of God to perform in them a good work unto completion. This is the basis of all confidence in the continuing nature of salvation. Thank you Lord for blessing us to have the conduct that others may see that will inspire confidence concerning our ultimate destiny that will draw others to Christ. We are so thankful and so grateful that He has started a good work in us. Blessings

95

Good Morning!

Then He said to them all, "If anyone desires to come after Me, let him deny himself, and take up his cross daily, and follow Me. 24 For whoever desires to save his life will lose it, but whoever loses his life for My sake will save it. **Luke**

The disciples of Jesus are those of us who have given our lives to Him and we will be obedient to our master even if it leads to hardship, persecution and death. We will no longer rule our own lives, but will deny our personal desires in order to please Jesus. In sacrificing the life that puts self first, we will find our only true life. Lord we thank you for blessing us to understand that Christ's death was an absolute requirement and precondition for human redemption. We are forever grateful unto our Lord and Savior. Blessings

96

Good Morning!

What then shall we say to these things?
If God is for us, who can be against us?
Romans

If God be for us who can be against us? The One who is infinitely wise has promised to direct us, the One who is infinitely good has promised to save us. What cunning strength or malice can prevail against His wisdom, power, and goodness? None. So, those of us who love Him are safe not only will we not have any essential damage by the persecution of ungodly individuals because even their attempted attacks will be working together for our good. All glory to God for being such a magnificent protector. Blessings

97 Good Morning!

I say then: Walk in the Spirit, and you shall not fulfill the lust of the flesh. **Galatians**

Sooner or later Christians find that we don't always do the good that our consciences tell us to do, because our sinful human nature fights against God's Spirit within us. The way we triumph over these wrong desires is not by putting ourselves under the law, but by allowing God's Spirit to direct our lives. Thank You Lord for reminding us of one of the statues of nature. If we live and subject ourselves to the influences of the Holy Spirit within us, we won't have any need to fear the power of the sensual and corrupt propensities of our carnal nature. We are grateful. Blessings

98 *Good Morning!*

As the deer pants for the water brooks, So pants my soul for You, O God. **Psalms**

This psalm can be likened to the prayer of a believer who wrestled and struggled with doubt and depression, but finally rested his case with God. Or maybe someone who has been pursued, spent, and ready to give up, but he turns and pants for God, for the living God, for the only wise God who can give life, who can give strength and the only one who can save us from death. He is the one who sees us through all of our disappointments and all of our negative situations and circumstances because our God will keep us safe and secure from all hurt, harm, and danger. We give Him all the glory. Blessings

99 Good Morning!

I can do all things through Christ who strengthens me. **Philippians**

We can flourish, we can be poor, whatever state we are in, we can do all things through Christ who strengthens us. The Lord had to prove this to us. We have lived as if there was something we could do worthwhile in our flesh. So we have tried too long to offer to God the sacrifices of our flesh. But thank God, after years of struggling, the Holy Spirit brought us to the truth of the statement of Christ and we realized the depth of it, apart from Him we can do nothing. Thank You Lord for reminding us that it is Christ who gives us the strength necessary to cope with the situations and circumstances of life that often threaten to overtake us. Through Him all things are possible. Blessings

100

Good Morning!

Behold, I send you out as sheep in the midst of wolves. Therefore be wise as serpents and harmless as doves. **Matthew**

Although they preached good news and did good works, the apostles could expect persecution. If brought to trial, whether before Jewish leaders or government officials, they would have the help of God's Spirit in giving them the right words to say. We need to maintain a reverent obedience to God, knowing that as our heavenly Father He will watch over us. He never forsakes those who are faithful to Him. We are grateful to have Him consistently watching over us. Blessings

101 *Good Morning!*

Do not cast me away from Your presence, And do not take Your Holy Spirit from me. 12 Restore to me the joy of Your salvation, And uphold me by Your generous Spirit. **Psalms**

When we sin against God if there is any godly sorrow, any feeling of regret or any desire to seek mercy, then our case is not hopeless because these things prove that the light of the Spirit has not been removed from us. The thing that David fears most is being separated from God this should be our greatest fear also. So, after he messed up, David asked God for a new heart, one that was free of sin, so that he might enjoy God's presence and obey God's law as he was created to do. Father, this is our prayer today. Lord thank You for Your merciful forgiveness, thank You for restoration so that we might enjoy Your loving kindness even when we have sinned against You, thank You Lord for peace of mind on this day. Blessings

102

Good Morning!

"Now, therefore," says the Lord, "Turn to Me with all your heart, With fasting, with weeping, and with mourning." 13 So rend your heart, and not your garments; Return to the Lord your God, For He is gracious and merciful, Slow to anger, and of great kindness; And He relents from doing harm. **Joel**

Although God is the one who has sent the judgment, it is not too late for people to ask for His mercy. However, this must be accompanied by genuine inward repentance, not just by the outward show of torn clothing, sackcloth and ashes. When we repent, God will restore our land and we will be able to worship him with our best offering again. God's repentance is a change of His will toward us and it is the result of a change of will and conduct on our part. Our repentance will cause God to pour out abundant blessing instead of judgment. We are eternally grateful. Blessings

103 *Good Morning!*

and the peace of God, which surpasses all understanding, will guard your hearts and minds through Christ Jesus. **Philippians**

This peace passes all understanding, it is of a very different nature from all that can arise from human occurrences, it is a peace that Christ has purchased, and God dispenses, it is felt by all the truly godly, but can be explained by none, it is communion with the Father, and His Son Jesus Christ, by the power and influence of the Holy Ghost. So, as we begin anew each day, let's remember that above all things, we must rejoice and be patient with one another at all times. We must learn not to worry but to pray with thankful and believing hearts. God's peace will then protect us from unnecessary mental and emotional tension. By filling our minds with the things that are good and honorable, we will have conduct that is good and honorable all the days of our lives. We are grateful. Blessings

104

Good Morning!

But you, beloved, building yourselves up on your most holy faith, praying in the Holy Spirit, 21 keep yourselves in the love of God, looking for the mercy of our Lord Jesus Christ unto eternal life. **Jude**

Our foundation is built on faith. Our expectations are met and exceeded by seeking all things from Christ who is our sum and substance for all the grace and glory we will need in this life. In order to strengthen our foundation, we must pray in the Spirit, holding fast to the divine influence that we have received. Remember, a prayer that is not sent up through the influence of the Holy Spirit is never likely to reach heaven. Lord, we are grateful for the reminder to build ourselves up, and to pray under the unction of the Holy Spirit in order to keep ourselves in the love of God, we understand that in spite of all of our diligence, self-denial, and obedience, we must look for the mercy of our Lord and Savior to bring us to eternal life. Thank You Lord for strengthening our foundation of faith. Blessings

105 *Good Morning!*

Even there Your hand shall lead me,
And Your right hand shall hold me. **Psalms**

God knows all about us what we do, what we think, where we go and what we say. Being the Creator, God has perfect knowledge of those He created. He knows our innermost thoughts as well as our physical characteristics, and He has a detailed knowledge of our emotions especially the ones we haven't experienced yet. Lord we thank you for being our constant and our consistent companion, thank you for being light in the midst of our darkness, thank you for being our strength when we are at our weakest, thank you for being our healer when the report is not in our favor, thank you Lord for being there for us today, yesterday, and forever. We are grateful. Blessings

106 *Good Morning!*

Even there Your hand shall lead me, And Your right hand shall hold me. **Psalms**

God knows all about us what we do, what we think, where we go and what we say. Being the Creator, God has perfect knowledge of those He created. He knows our innermost thoughts as well as our physical characteristics, and He has a detailed knowledge of our emotions especially the ones we haven't experienced yet. Lord we thank you for being our constant and our consistent companion, thank you for being light in the midst of our darkness, thank you for being our strength when we are at our weakest, thank you for being our healer when the report is not in our favor, thank you Lord for being there for us today, yesterday, and forever. We are grateful. Blessings

107

Good Morning!

For do I now persuade men, or God? Or do I seek to please men? For if I still pleased men, I would not be a bondservant of Christ. **Galatians**

The Judaisers had accused Paul of not preaching circumcision, to make it easy for Gentiles to join the church. They were claiming that he preached to please people. He pronounced the curse of God on all who lived contrary to the one true gospel, twice to the people. By preaching the truth, Paul wanted to show that he wasn't trying to win someone's favor, his aim was to please Christ and win souls to Him. Paul emphasized that the gospel he preached was not of human invention and it didn't come from a human source. He wanted all to know that he received the word through the direct work of God in him. Thank you Lord for blessing Paul to be steadfast, transparent, and true to the gospel. We are grateful for his example. Blessings

108

Good Morning!

Commit your works to the Lord, And your thoughts will be established. **Proverbs**

Let's strive to make sure that whatever we do is commanded by God, meaning all things should begin, continue, and end in His name. Then He will establish our thoughts. So the plans we have in our heart will be agreeable to His divine will. God's thoughts and mediations are already established so all of the issues of our heart will align with His plans and all will be well with us. Remember, we make our plans, but God determines the outcome. He is well aware of our unseen motives so He controls events according to His purpose. Thank you Lord for reminding us to always include You in our plans so that our thoughts will be established and we will stay in Your will. We are grateful. Blessings

109

Good Morning!

Be kindly affectionate to one another with brotherly love, in honor giving preference to one another **Romans**

We must strive to consider all of our brothers and sisters as more worthy than ourselves and we can't let grief or envy affect our mind when we see others being honored and we appear to always be neglected. This is a very hard lesson and very few individuals learn it thoroughly. Lord thank you for reminding us that we need to be sincere and straightforward in everything we do. We should always display a loving care for those who are our fellow members of the body of Christ. We are so grateful to God for this reminder. Blessings

110

Good Morning!

Search me, O God, and know my heart; Try me, and know my anxieties; 24 And see if there is any wicked way in me, And lead me in the way everlasting. **Psalms**

Through our meditation of the word, we should be growing so close to God that we see the wicked as God sees them and we should hate evil as God hates it. So we should always pray that God will act in righteous judgment towards us. Even though we know that we have fallen short and also are far from perfect, in the midst of our imperfections, we are so thankful and so grateful that we serve a God who will show us our sin, cleanse us, and lead us into a life of holiness. Lord we are so appreciative of Your faithfulness, guidance, and direction as you lead us to the way of everlasting life. Blessings

111

Good Morning!

"For I have satiated the weary soul, and I have replenished every sorrowful soul." **Jeremiah**

Jeremiah had a vision of Jerusalem as a city of righteousness and Judah as a land of contentment. This is a vision that gave him the satisfaction of a pleasant dream. The people were facing their destruction, but in the midst of that God took His prophet beyond the dark period that they were currently experiencing straight to the end of their experience so that he could see the glorious restoration of God's grace and love that He had for His people. This is just a reminder for all of us who are in the midst of our storm to keep holding on to His unchanging hand. We may have done some things to get ourselves into this devastating and destructive place or we may have just been called to experience life as we have never done so before. The test doesn't matter because we serve a God who specializes in restoration so be encouraged on this day regardless of the season that we are in, He's going to bring us out stronger, better, and more spiritually grounded than we have ever been before because He wants us to also see His glorious restoration of grace and love in our lives. Blessings

112

Good Morning!

Put on the whole armor of God, that you may be able to stand against the wiles of the devil. **Ephesians**

In our warfare against the wiles of the devil, we are to arm ourselves with spiritual armor against the methods of the devil just like the Roman soldiers so that the devil won't have an opportunity to cast through when we least expect him. Lord thank You for the whole armor, we humbly come before You asking that You will give us the strength, the courage, and most definitely the skill to use it in the way that You have intended. We are eternally grateful. Blessings

113

Good Morning!

And let us consider one another in order to stir up love and good works, 25 not forsaking the assembling of ourselves together, as is the manner of some, but exhorting one another, and so much the more as you see the Day approaching. **Hebrews**

Early Christians had a fellowship that drew them together for worship and preparation. The author of Hebrews is reminding us that this practice of assembling together needs to increase within the believing community today because the day of Christ is quickly approaching. This passage provides one of the strongest affirmations in the Bible of the crucial importance of the local church and the necessity pressed upon every Christian to be faithful to a local church of faithful saints. Thank you Lord for allowing us to gather together for mutual encouragement, the strengthening of each other, and to exhort one another in Jesus name. Amen. Blessings

114

Good Morning!

Fear not, for I am with you; Be not dismayed, for I am your God. I will strengthen you, Yes, I will help you, I will uphold you with My righteous right hand.'
Isaiah

The people of Israel are the people of the living God. Just like He chose them, He has chosen us and He has not forgotten us. He is always present to strengthen and protect us. Lord, we are so thankful and so grateful to have You watching over us. Blessings

115

Good Morning!

But Jesus looked at them and said to them, "With men this is impossible, but with God all things are possible." **Matthew**

Wealth makes people independent of others and so the rich often find it difficult to acknowledge that they are not independent of God. The accumulation of wealth doesn't make them any better in God's sight than anyone else. Because of their wealth, few of the rich enter the kingdom of God. In actuality, no one can enter the kingdom apart from the work of God. Thankfully, by His grace He accepts those who humble themselves before Him. All Christians have an imperious sense of need, for example, when a man has many things on earth, he is in danger of thinking that he does not need God; when a man has few things on earth, he is driven to God because he has nowhere else to go. Thank You Lord for allowing us to humbly submit to You and Your will as we accept Your offer of eternal life. We are grateful. Blessings

116

Good Morning!

1 I waited patiently for the Lord; And He inclined to me, And heard my cry. 2 He also brought me up out of a horrible pit, Out of the miry clay, And set my feet upon a rock, And established my steps. **Psalms**

In this verse, David magnifies God for giving him the mercy he asked for. It is a thanksgiving for his recovery from the disease that had afflicted him in his body. He also shows God that he is grateful for his restoration to Divine favor. When we are in the pit, where nothing can be heard except the howlings of wild beasts, or the hollow sounds of the winds all around us, He faithfully delivers us. When we are in the miry clay sinking deeper and deeper in a position where we can't save ourselves, in the midst of these trials, God changes our state from guilt to pardon or from corruption to holiness. After this, we have power over all sin, and we can walk upright and steady in the way that leads to God's kingdom. Thank You Lord for hearing our cry, setting our feet on the solid rock, and establishing our steps in Your will. We are eternally grateful. Blessings

117

Good Morning!

Therefore submit to God. Resist the devil and he will flee from you. **James**

We must submit to God, continue to bow to all His decisions, and to all His dispensations. We must strive to resist the devil, he cannot conquer us if we continue to resist him. Strong as he is, God never permits him to conquer the individual who continues to resist him, regardless of what we think or see, the enemy cannot force the human will. God has given believers the Holy Spirit to control our lives and He wants no rivals, such as the spirit of worldliness, to turn us away from Him. Lord thank you for strengthening us who, in our humility, draw near to You and resist the enemy's temptations to have us rely on worldly methods. We are eternally grateful to have Your Holy Spirit guiding us along the way. Blessings

118 Good Morning!

A man's heart plans his way,
But the Lord directs his steps.
Proverbs

We may make plans, but God is the one who determines the outcome. He knows our unseen motives and controls events according to His purposes. It is important for us to always bring God into our planning. Lord we want You to stop us whenever we are getting out of line and doing something that isn't from You and directed by You. We want You to interrupt us. We want You to disturb us because we want You to always direct our steps and guide us along the right way. We are grateful. Blessings

119

Good Morning!

Then Jesus said to His disciples, "If anyone desires to come after Me, let him deny himself, and take up his cross, and follow Me. **Matthew**

The principles of the Christian life are first, to have a sincere desire to belong to Christ. Secondly, to renounce self-dependence, and selfish pursuits and thirdly, to embrace the condition which God has appointed, and bear the troubles and difficulties we may meet while walking the Christian road. As disciples of Jesus we have given our lives to Jesus, and we will be obedient to our master even if it leads to hardship, persecution and death. We will no longer rule our own lives, but we will deny our personal desires in order to please Jesus. In sacrificing the life that puts self first, we will find the only true life. On the other hand those who live for themselves may gain what they want in the present world, but they will lose the only life of lasting value, eternal life. Thank You Lord for an opportunity to take up our cross and follow You. Blessings

120 — Good Morning!

Therefore, having been justified by faith, we have peace with God through our Lord Jesus Christ, **Romans**

Paul's conclusion may be broken down into three main points: (1) All are in need of "justification" (this is because all have sinned), (2) Justification is by faith instead of meritorious works and/or flawless law keeping, (3) Justification must come through Jesus Christ. Justification means the saved are freed from the penalty of sin and are the recipients of grace and other spiritual blessings. Lord thank you for justifying us so that we may experience peace with You through our Lord and Savior. Blessings

121

Good Morning!

Yours, O Lord, is the greatness, The power and the glory, The victory and the majesty; For all that is in heaven and in earth is Yours; Yours is the kingdom, O Lord, And You are exalted as head over all.
I Chronicles

Lord, it's all yours. You're the One who has given riches. You're the One who gives power. You're the One who gives abilities and everything else. It all belongs to You. So, all that we have done is give You that which is really Yours. Thank You Lord for the opportunity to bless Your Holy name and give You honor and glory for being the Ruler of all things. Blessings

122

Good Morning!

Let the words of my mouth and the meditation of my heart Be acceptable in Your sight, O Lord, my strength and my Redeemer. **Psalms**

Lord thank You for reminding us of the necessity of us to be governed by the Holy Spirit, in order to regulate our life uprightly and honestly. By the word acceptable, David shows us that the only rule of living well is for us to strive to please God, and to be approved by Him. Lord because You are our Strength and our Redeemer, please cleanse our life so we that we will be acceptable to You. We are grateful. Blessings

123

Good Morning!

No temptation has overtaken you except such as is common to man; but God is faithful, who will not allow you to be tempted beyond what you are able, but with the temptation will also make the way of escape, that you may be able to bear it. **I Corinthians**

Tests and temptations will most definitely come, but we will always have a way of escape. We won't have any excuses during this season of our lives because we will always have God in our corner and He is forever faithful and completely loyal. With God, we can bear anything. Thank You Lord. Blessings

124

Good Morning!

And my God shall supply all your need according to His riches in glory by Christ Jesus. **Philippians**

As we offer our gifts and sacrifices to God, He treats them like an investment, and He is our banker who has the power to add interest to our account. Because of our gifts, sacrifices, and obedience, we have more than enough. All who trust God and do His will, are being strategically positioned to be repaid according to His abundant wealth in Jesus Christ. Thank You Lord for always making sure we have more than enough. We are grateful. Blessings

125

Good Morning!

Do not remember the former things, Nor consider the things of old. 19 Behold, I will do a new thing, Now it shall spring forth; Shall you not know it? I will even make a road in the wilderness And rivers in the desert. **Isaiah**

Lord, thank you for reminding us that as the old things pass away, you are doing a new thing in our lives and you are allowing many new things to come to pass, but the blessed part is that you are telling us of the new things before you bring them to pass. We need to pay attention with our spiritual sense because so many of us are missing our blessings based on what we see in the natural. Stop grumbling and complaining about what is placed before you, a greater blessing is often hidden in the midst of what has been presented to you. Trust God because He's still making roads in the wilderness and creating rivers in the desert. Blessings

126

Good Morning!

Cause me to hear Your lovingkindness in the morning, For in You do I trust; Cause me to know the way in which I should walk, For I lift up my soul to You. **Psalms**

Sometimes our prayer is one that asks God to hear us so that He might answer by the morning so that we can hear His loving kindness in the response. Because of His faithfulness, we will trust Him even the more as He guides our steps in the way that He would have us to go. We are eternally grateful that we have a Heavenly Father we can lift our soul to as an offering of peace, love, obedience, and humility. Thank you Lord. Blessings

127 *Good Morning!*

Pursue peace with all people, and holiness, without which no one will see the Lord. **Hebrews**

We need to cultivate a good understanding, with all people and strive to pursue peace, kindness, and holiness with care and diligence. To see God is to enjoy Him, but without holiness in our heart and our life it will be impossible to see Him. We can do our part to help others see God by developing holiness among believers, by being an example of holiness, and by learning how to deal with those who show signs of bitterness one on one. Lord we thank You for the opportunity to seek peace and holiness in all things and we praise you for the opportunity to be the example of holiness that You have called us to be. We are eternally grateful. Blessings

128

Good Morning!

Now this is the confidence that we have in Him, that if we ask anything according to His will, He hears us. **I John**

All that God has promised we are justified in expecting and what he has promised we can inquire about in prayer. Prayer is the language of the children of God. Prayer is also the language of dependence on God. Faith and prayer should not be used to claim what we have asked God for, we must take heed that what we ask and believe for is agreeable to the revealed will of our God. What we know has been promised to us, we can freely plead for and know that He will answer. Thank You Lord for answering our prayers. Blessings

129

Good Morning!

Fight the good fight of faith, lay hold on eternal life, to which you were also called and have confessed the good confession in the presence of many witnesses.
1 Timothy

We have a contest to sustain in which our honor, our life, and our soul, are at stake. We should live the Gospel, and defend the cause of God. So, let's unmask the hypocrites, expel the profligate, purge and build up the Church, as we live in the spirit of our religion, and give ourselves fully to the work of the Lord. Thank you Lord for the opportunity to confess and acknowledge You in all our ways. Amen. Blessings

130

Good Morning!

The Lord is my rock and my fortress and my deliverer; My God, my strength, in whom I will trust; My shield and the horn of my salvation, my stronghold. **Psalms**

David began his praise by verbalizing his love for God for being so good to him. He proceeded to describe how much the Lord meant to him by using many metaphors. God was the source of his strength, stability, safety, and salvation. He was the one in whom David sought refuge, his defense, his power, and his protection. Because God had proved to be such a reliable Savior, David regarded Him worthy of his praise, we should be doing the same thing today. One of the greatest tragedies of the human spirit is to become a prisoner of ungratefulness, being ungrateful shuts the human spirit up in a world lightened only by self, and self has no light at all. We must not become complacent when God blesses us. Be grateful to Him in all things because only God can be our strength, stability, safety, and salvation all day, every day. Give Him glory for allowing you to lean on Him. Blessings

131

Good Morning!

In this the love of God was manifested toward us, that God has sent His only begotten Son into the world, that we might live through Him. **1 John 4:9 NKJV**

John is showing that love is grounded in God's nature. Those who have been born of God ought to emulate His character. God provides both the source and example of the believer's love. So love for others is an integral part of one's relationship with God. While no one has seen God. His love is evident in the work and in the believer's love for others. Let's strive to be the example of love that God has shown us, by releasing envy, hate, bitterness, and negativity because they are weighing us down and preventing us from elevating to the greater heights of love that God desires for our lives. Blessings

132

Good Morning!

Let your light so shine before men, that they may see your good works and glorify your Father in heaven. **Matthew 5:16 NKJV**

Just as a candle is not hidden but is put in a place where it gives light, Christians should not hide ourselves, we should strive to live and work in places where we can bring people to know and worship our God. It's not sufficient enough to just have light, we need to walk in the light, and by the light. Our whole conduct should be a perpetual comment on the doctrine we have received, and a constant exemplification of its power and truth. We are grateful that our God is glorified when the glorious power of His grace is manifested in the salvation of men. Let's strive to allow our light to shine before others so that they may be drawn to uplift, worship, and praise our Lord and Savior. Blessings

133 Good Morning!

Repent therefore and be converted, that your sins may be blotted out, so that times of refreshing may come from the presence of the Lord. **Acts 3:19 NKJV**

If the Jews repented of their sin in crucifying Jesus, God would forgive them. They would then experience all those blessings of the messianic age that they longed for and that the prophets of Old Testament times had spoken of. The climax of those blessings would be the return of Jesus Christ himself. Just like the Jews, we must repent of our sins because there are many blessings of the messianic age waiting for us to turn from our wicked ways. Repent and be baptized, He died for our freedom. Blessings

134

Good Morning!

whom God set forth as a propitiation by His blood, through faith, to demonstrate His righteousness, because in His forbearance God had passed over the sins that were previously committed. **Romans 3:25 NKJV**

Being holy, perfect, and immutable, the living God is never ruled by changing moods. Consequently, God's wrath is a settled disposition against evil. The just demands of God's holiness for the punishment and exclusion of sin must be satisfied. Propitiation is the work of Christ on the cross in which He met the demands of the righteousness of God against sin, both satisfying the requirements of God's justice and canceling the guilt of man. Christ's death on the cross propitiated God and reconciled man. We are eternally grateful. Blessings

135 — Good Morning!

For the earth will be filled
With the knowledge of the glory of
the Lord, As the waters cover the sea.
Habakkuk 2:14 NKJV

This verse explains God's power and providence and how it is widely displayed in the destruction of Babylon and its empire, and the humiliation of Nebuchadnezzar, and in the captivity and restoration of its people. Secondly, it may be applied to the glorious days of the Messiah and the land of Judea will be filled with the knowledge of God. God's great design fully discovered, and the scheme of salvation amply explained. Lastly, the earth cannot perish until every continent, island, and inhabitant, has been illuminated with the light of the Gospel of our Lord and Savior, Jesus Christ. Lord, we give you all the glory. Amen. Blessings

136

Good Morning!

Trust in the Lord with all your heart,
And lean not on your own understanding; 6
In all your ways acknowledge Him,
And He shall direct your paths.
Proverbs 3:5-6 NKJV

These verses express a firm admonition and gracious assurance for us. Throughout proverbs we see the reward of trusting in or literally clinging to God with the idea of setting our hope and confidence on the Him as opposed to the uselessness of resting in our own wisdom and seeking our own way. God designed us, His creation, to have a dependency on Him. Even our ordinary decisions of each day, need the counsel of God. He instructs us to consult Him about the most minute details, whether in the spiritual or the secular realm, He promises to communicate in return. The Fall itself was caused by man seeking to live independently of God, unfortunately, this human independence continues at the heart of sinful rebellion today. Lord teach us how to trust You, seek You, and acknowledge You in all things, rid us Lord of the rebellion that lives beneath the surface of our heart. We are grateful. Blessings

137

Good Morning!

For I know the thoughts that I think toward you, says the Lord, thoughts of peace and not of evil,
to give you a future and a hope.
Jeremiah 29:11 NKJV

God is indirectly condemning the Jews, because they entertained no hope of deliverance except from what came within the reach of their senses. He then teaches us that true wisdom is to obey God, and to surrender ourselves to Him so when we don't understand His plan, we will patiently wait until our season of prosperity comes. We can only do this by trusting the thoughts He has for us. Blessings

138

Good Morning!

Therefore do not worry about tomorrow, for tomorrow will worry about its own things. Sufficient for the day is its own trouble. **Matthew 6:34 NKJV**

The future time which God would have us foresee and provide for is that of judgment and eternity and it is about this alone that we are careless. Each day has its own peculiar trials, we should meet them with confidence in God. We can only live one day at a time, so we should take care to suffer no more evils in one day than are necessarily attached to it. All who neglect the present for the future are acting opposite to the order of God, your own interest, and to every dictate of sound wisdom. Let's strive to live for eternity, and we will secure all that is valuable in due time. Blessings

139

Good Morning!

A new commandment I give to you, that you love one another; as I have loved you, that you also love one another.
John 13:34 NKJV

The death of Jesus brought glory to God by displaying His immeasurable love for sinful men and women. It would also bring grief to His disciples as they saw their master taken from them. But they were to show no bitterness in their grief, instead they were to have forgiving love in their hearts so that others would see that they were indeed disciples of Jesus. Thank you Lord for reminding us to love one another as You have loved us. Amen... blessings

140

Good Morning!

I will instruct you and teach you in the way you should go; I will guide you with My eye.
Psalm 32:8 NKJV

Up until now David has been speaking of God and his relationship to God, but in this verse God responds to David, and David writes God's response to him. I will give you all the assistance you require, I will become your Instructor, and I will teach you, in all things, the way you should go. I will keep my eyes upon you, and you shall keep yours upon me, as I go, you must follow me, and I will continually watch for your good. Thank you Lord for instructing us, teaching us, and always being a positive example before us. We are grateful. Blessings

141

Good Morning!

And when they had prayed, the place where they were assembled together was shaken; and they were all filled with the Holy Spirit, and they spoke the word of God with boldness. **Acts 4:31 NKJV**

In this scripture, we have been shown the threefold result of the prayer of the apostles after the church was delivered from the Sanhedrin- the place where they chose to assemble was shaken, they were all filled with the Holy Spirit, and they were given the ability to speak the word of God with boldness. This filling of the Holy Spirit was a fresh in-filling comparable to their filling of the Holy Spirit on the Day of Pentecost. This was our God refueling His servants according their needs in a new situation. At the time of this prayer, they needed boldness and that is what they received. Thank you Lord for always answering our prayers, thank you for making the path of prayer and thanksgiving plain for us to follow. We are grateful. Blessings

142

Good Morning!

You are of God, little children, and have overcome them, because He who is in you is greater than he who is in the world. **I John**

Greater is He that is within me than he that is in the world. Thank God for the Holy Spirit who lives in us. We have overcome by the blood of the Lamb and we are grateful. God cares for those of us who trust in Him, this will assure us the victory over the enemy because He lives on the inside of us. All glory to God. Blessings

143 *Good Morning!*

Death and life are in the power of the tongue, And those who love it will eat its fruit. **Proverbs 19:21 NKJV**

Words can bring life, joy, encouragement, hope and healing when delivered in the right tone and at the right time. Likewise our words can humiliate and destroy others if we don't carefully monitor them and control their use. Out of the abundance of the heart the mouth speaks. The good person out of his good treasure brings forth good, and the evil person out of his evil treasure brings forth evil. What are you bringing forth? Blessings

144

Good Morning!

And you shall know the truth,
and the truth shall make you free.
John

By knowing the truth, we will have a constant experimental knowledge of its power and efficacy. The truth will make us free because the bondage of sin is the most grievous bondage and having the opportunity to experience freedom from the guilt and influence of being bound is the greatest freedom. The only one who can free us is God, acting through His Son Jesus. With Him on our side, we will find our true freedom through faith in Jesus and continual obedience to His teachings. We are grateful. Blessings

145 Good Morning!

A man who has friends must himself be friendly, But there is a friend who sticks closer than a brother. **Proverbs**

If we don't maintain a friendly disposition we cannot expect to keep our friends. Friendship is a good plant, but it requires cultivation to make it grow. In many cases, the genuine friend shows more attachment and adds greater value to our lives than our natural brother. Our fake friends will be in our corner during prosperity, but a true friend is consistently united closely to us even in the most disastrous circumstances. True friendship is not easily broken and it doesn't make a distinction between the richer partner and the poorer partner. Thank you Lord for my true friend. Blessings

146

Good Morning!

And those who are Christ's have crucified the flesh with its passions and desires. **Galatians**

Our lives should demonstrate the truth that our sinful nature has been crucified with Christ and has no further power over us. We are now under the influence of God's spirit. Lord thank You for helping us to understand that the corrupt passions of our soul have been been put to death or destroyed and they no longer have any power over us. We are so grateful for the Holy Spirit. Blessings

147

Good Morning!

This Book of the Law shall not depart from your mouth, but you shall meditate in it day and night, that you may observe to do according to all that is written in it. For then you will make your way prosperous, and then you will have good success.
Joshua 1:8 NKJV

Sometimes we misunderstand what it means, to prosper which has given rise to prosperity teaching that places the emphasis on temporal, worldly prosperity rather than eternal spiritual wealth. God may choose to give worldly wealth to His children or He may allow the alternative, we need to learn how to be content in whatever God allows. It's important for us to know the Word of God, to trust His Word, and to apply the Word in every circumstance of life, knowing, to do so will lead to success in our Christian life because all things work together for good to those that love the Lord and trust His Word. Blessings

148

Good Morning!

If we live in the Spirit,
let us also walk in the Spirit.
Galatians 5:25 NKJV

As we strive to live in the spirit, because the Holy Spirit lives, and breathes inside of us, we need to allow the spirit to go before us, so that we can walk in the spirit under the guidance of holiness. The Holy Spirit is a part of us He will guide us, He will direct us, He will correct us, and He will lead us down the right path if we let Him. Lord, thank you for your Holy Spirit that lives inside of us and keeps us on the narrow path. Blessings

149

Good Morning!

Surely goodness and mercy shall follow me All the days of my life; And I will dwell in the house of the Lord Forever. **Psalm 23:6 NKJV**

Because the Lord is our shepherd, we are confident that His goodness and mercy follows us all the days of our lives. Because He loves us and His goodness and mercy follows us in every circumstance, at the end of this life, we are assured that we will enter heaven, the house of the Lord, and we will live there forever. All glory to God for His promises and His consistent faithfulness in our lives. Amen. Blessings

150 Good Morning!

Rejoice always, 17 pray without ceasing, 18 in everything give thanks; for this is the will of God in Christ Jesus for you.
1 Thessalonians 5:16-18 NKJV

As we follow Christ, we should experience joy, in spite of the hard times. We should continually be praying with thoughts of His goodness reminding us His mercy. And let's not forget to always be thankful for what God has done, and is doing, for us. Lord, thank You for Your faithfulness. Blessings

151

Good Morning!

Oh, give thanks to the Lord,
for He is good!
For His mercy endures forever.
Psalm 107:1 NKJV

On this day that the world has set aside to show thanks, we pause to lift up the name of our Lord, the One we need to thank first, for His faithfulness, His grace, and His tender mercies that endure forever. We honor Him on this day of thanksgiving. Blessings

152

Good Morning!

Let the word of Christ dwell in you richly in all wisdom, teaching and admonishing one another in psalms and hymns and spiritual songs, singing with grace in your hearts to the Lord. **Colossians 3:16 NKJV**

Thank you, God, for manufacturing the word of Christ in our hearts. If we let it, Christ's word can instruct and teach us. At the same time, Christ's word can also show us where we are wrong. Paul is reminding us that all types of music should be used to let the word of Christ dwell richly within us. Our singing is to be done with an attitude of thanksgiving. Singing praises to God is largely associated with showing our gratitude to Him, rather than focusing on ourselves or our own desires. We are grateful for the word of God and the many ways that it blesses us. Amen. Blessings

153

Good Morning!

The Lord bless you and keep you; 25 The Lord make His face shine upon you, And be gracious to you; 26 The Lord lift up His countenance upon you, And give you peace." **Numbers 6:24-26 NKJV**

Our God loves us so much that He blesses us beyond measure and He keeps us safe. He allows His face to shine upon us and He extends His grace to us because He cares for us. He lifts up His eyes and He scrutinizes our lives and extends His peace to us as we move about in our daily tests and trials. He is mighty, He is gracious, He is our keeper, and He gives us peace. We are grateful. Blessings

154

Good Morning!

There is no fear in love; but perfect love casts out fear, because fear involves torment. But he who fears has not been made perfect in love.
1 John 4:18 NKJV

When we experience God's love in our lives and share it with others, we don't need to fear. The perfect love of Christ teaches us how to walk in an upright and righteous manner, so torment won't be associated with us in eternity. Because we have a relationship with God based on His love for us, we are confident and secure as we follow His will for our lives. Thank you Lord. We are grateful. Blessings

155

Good Morning!

As every man hath received the gift, even so minister the same one to another, as good stewards of the manifold grace of God. **1 Peter 4:10 NKJV**

We need to manage our minds for effective praying and show genuine to one another this includes sharing our homes and food with Christians who are in need. We need to understand that whatever we have is a gift from God. Because all that we have, has been given to us by our Lord. Wisely using everything we have to serve each other is part of fulfilling our purpose as God's set-apart people. Blessings

156

Good Morning!

So let each one give as he purposes in his heart, not grudgingly or of necessity; for God loves a cheerful giver.
2 Corinthians 9:7 NKJV

God increases the ability of believers who give generously to give even more. This results in increasing His righteousness on earth, and it creates a sense of gratitude and thankfulness to Him for overflow. We are so thankful and so grateful that God is glorified for giving us the gift of giving and we pray for those who give in humble submission to His will, expecting nothing in return. Blessings

157

Good Morning!

Every good gift and every perfect gift is from above, and comes down from the Father of lights, with whom there is no variation or shadow of turning.
James 1:17 NKJV

It's important for us to cling to the truth, which is that every good thing in our lives is a gift from God. Where did all those good things come from? James is encouraging believers in Christ to tell themselves the truth: God gave you every single good thing in your life. He is the source of all the good we have and all the good we crave. Who God is does not change when our circumstances change. Lord thank You. Blessings

158

Good Morning!

Blessed are those who keep His testimonies, Who seek Him with the whole heart! **Psalm 119:2 NKJV**

This verse reminds us that blessed are those who keep His statutes and seek Him with all their hearts. We have to understand that we are indeed blessed if we keep the Word of God inside us. After all, He is our shield, He is our Provider, He is our strength, and He is our salvation. Let's strive to always seek Him wholeheartedly. Amen. Blessings

159

Good Morning!

For if you forgive men their trespasses, your heavenly Father will also forgive you.
Matthew 6:14 NKJV

This means we should ask God for forgiveness, as we declare our forgiveness of those who have wronged us. What Christ is teaching here is that forgiveness is conditional, but only in a specific sense. If we forgive the sins of others against us, Jesus is saying our heavenly Father will also forgive us. If we don't forgive, we won't be forgiven. How difficult is it for you to forgive? Blessings

160

Good Morning!

Therefore lay aside all filthiness and overflow of wickedness, and receive with meekness the implanted word, which is able to save your souls. **James 1:21 NKJV**

James continues to describe what it looks like to truly trust God. How does that show up in our daily lives? By trusting God and rejecting sin. Sin is what happens when we choose to serve ourselves first, and above all. James doesn't tell us to stop sinning and just be better people. He tells us to stop sinning and accept, or accept on a deeper level, the message of Christ, with humility.
It is Christ's goodness in us that counts, not our own efforts to be good. Christ in us is what will save our souls. Lord we are grateful. Amen. Blessings

161

Good Morning!

Sanctify them by Your truth.
Your word is truth.
John 17:17 NKJV

What God tells us through the person, the teaching, and the message of Christ is that which is real. It is actual; it is "truth" in the deepest and most fundamental sense. God is truth, and salvation comes when we accept the reality of who He is, and who we are. Thank you God for setting us apart to be used for Your glory and placing Your word deep within us. We are grateful. Blessings

162

Good Morning!

But those who wait on the Lord Shall renew their strength; They shall mount up with wings like eagles, They shall run and not be weary, They shall walk and not faint.
Isaiah 40:31 NKJV

The path of the righteous requires patience and waiting on the future glory of Christ to be revealed. The waiting doesn't mean we are stagnant, this is our time of strengthening. The strength that we gain during the waiting process prepares us to make it through our trials and temptations. It prepares us to do righteous acts to honor our Lord and Savior who brings us to the good that He has promised us. So as we prepare to mount up on wings as eagles, let's run this race, we will not be weary, we will not faint because our strength comes from on high. All glory to God. Amen. Blessings

163

Good Morning!

And you will seek Me and find Me when you search for Me with all your heart. **Jeremiah 29:13 NKJV**

We all have a desire to be noticed on some level or by someone, we want to be understood, we want to feel valued, and we want to feel at home wherever we are in life. Remember when we feel out of place, pushed aside or passed over, call on the Savior because God is always listening to us. So let's seek Him and diligently search for Him with all our heart. In this scripture, He is reminding us of His presence and His promise to keep us safe and to always bring us home. We are grateful. Blessings

164

Good Morning!

Be strong and of good courage, do not fear nor be afraid of them; for the Lord your God, He is the One who goes with you. He will not leave you nor forsake you.
Deuteronomy 31:6 NKJV

The strength and courage that we have, is woven into the fabric of our lives before we are formed in our mother's womb. We don't have to fear or be afraid of anything because the Lord is with us. We are equipped to embrace courage and strength, not because of our own abilities or resources, but because we know that He is with us. We are grateful because He has promised to never leave us nor forsake us as we are called to endure the tests and trials of this life. Blessings

165

Good Morning!

But sanctify the Lord God in your hearts, and always be ready to give a defense to everyone who asks you a reason for the hope that is in you, with meekness and fear. **1 Peter 3:15 NKJV**

We need to strive to live as if Christ is our Master and even during our times of suffering, we are called to fully submit to our Lord and Savior. In the midst of our suffering, our hope should be apparent. So, be ready to answer the question our lives should inspire: "How can you be so hopeful in the midst of difficult circumstances?"

Thank you Lord, for setting aside a place in our heart to worship and celebrate you. We are grateful. Blessings

166

Good Morning!

Let us hold fast the confession of our hope without wavering, for He who promised is faithful. **Hebrews 10:23 NKJV**

We are called to hold fast without wavering because of our hope. This means we're immovable and unbending. The idea is that we don't compromise, we don't surrender and we don't move. We must hold on to the unchanging hand of our Lord and Savior without moving. Thank you Lord, for blessed assurance, we are grateful. Blessings

167

Good Morning!

The Lord takes pleasure in those who fear Him, In those who hope in His mercy.
Psalm 147:11 NKJV

The Lord takes pleasure in those of us who fear Him. Those who are truly religious and righteous. In this our hope is His mercy. We seeking the salvation of our souls. But the blessed part of this is, even the cry of those who are wrong and sorrowful is pleasing in the ear of our Lord. We are grateful. Blessings

168

Good Morning!

And now abide faith, hope, love, these three; but the greatest of these is love.
1 Corinthians 13:13 NKJV

We must have all three of these abiding or remaining in us as children of the Most High God. Faith is essential to Christians, hope is our conviction that Gods is a promise keeper. Love will remain even after our faith has been fulfilled and our hope in eternity is a true realization. All that we do, must be done in love, if it's not, it means nothing and that can be destructive to our lives. Thank you Lord for faith, hope, and love. Blessings

169

Good Morning!

The voice of one crying in the wilderness: "Prepare the way of the Lord; Make straight in the desert A highway for our God. **Isaiah 40:3 NKJV**

This scripture is reminding us of the common practice of monarchs, who, before traveling into a new place, would send people ahead of them to make sure that the road, the way, was passable. The path to righteousness started with one man, Jesus, we are to follow those ahead of us who are continuing to follow Him. The path has already been cleared, bridges have been constructed, hills have been leveled, and the holes have been filled. We just need to take up our cross and follow. Blessings

170

Good Morning!

Therefore I say to you, do not worry about your life, what you will eat or what you will drink; nor about your body, what you will put on. Is not life more than food and the body more than clothing?
Matthew 6:25 NKJV

This verse reminds us of why we should not be over anxious about material things. Let's not obsess over wealth, we should strive to focus on godly, eternal rewards. It's worth the effort. Amen. Blessings

171

Good Morning!

"Whoever confesses that Jesus is the Son of God, God dwelleth in him, and he in God." **John.**

Here, John is teaching us that the person who confesses that Jesus is God's Son has God living in him, and that person lives in God. John has now shifted from recognizing Jesus in others to recognizing Jesus in one's own life. Jesus is both fully human and fully divine. We may not fully understand it, but we must recognize Jesus as both human and divine. Without His humanity, He could not die and rise again. Without His deity, He could not be without sin and offer Himself as a perfect sacrifice. Both aspects of His being are essential to His work and to our salvation. Lord thank you for the deity and humanity of Christ. We glorify you for abiding in us. Amen. Blessings

172

Good Morning!

Oh come, let us worship and bow down;
Let us kneel before the Lord our Maker.
Psalm 95:6 NKJV

We need God's mercy and our Savior's sacrifice to forgive us and cleanse us, we need to humbly bow before Him, our Maker. It's an honor to worship such a worthy Father. Seeking Him first gives us assurance of no longer being bound or subdued by our sins and failures. We are free to serve the One who is worthy of all the praise, the glory, and the honor. Only He is due such goodness. We are grateful for every opportunity to serve Him. Blessings

173

Good Morning!

He who has My commandments and keeps them, it is he who loves Me. And he who loves Me will be loved by My Father, and I will love him and manifest Myself to him. **John 14:21 NKJV**

The Holy Spirit is in every believer. Our ability to follow the will of God depends on the influence of His Spirit. A person's obedience to Christ's teaching is evidence that they have faith in Him. Good works cannot produce salvation, but salvation will produce an attitude of obedience. Lord we are so grateful for the manifestation of You and Your everlasting love in our lives. Blessings

174

Good Morning!

But you, beloved, building yourselves up on your most holy faith, praying in the Holy Spirit, 21 keep yourselves in the love of God, looking for the mercy of our Lord Jesus Christ unto eternal life.
Jude 1:20-21 NKJV

This is how we maintain our life with God. For today's believer, defense against false teaching starts with growing in the knowledge and applying the Scripture. God gave the Scriptures to make us wise regarding salvation and spiritual maturity. But prayer, inspired and empowered by the Holy Spirit, should also accompany our loyalty to God's Word Let's strive to build on our faith through prayer as we seek the love and mercy of God for eternity. All glory to God. Blessings

175

Good Morning!

But as He who called you is holy, you also be holy in all your conduct
1 Peter 1:15 NKJV

God wants us to be set apart from sin to His righteousness. God does not want us to be ordinary. He wants us to fashion our lives after His glorious example. Blessings

176

Good Morning!

Now may the God of hope fill you with all joy and peace in believing, that you may abound in hope by the power of the Holy Spirit. **Roman's 15:13 NKJV**

Thank you Lord for being our God of hope, thank you for filling us with joy and peace to believe that we can thrive in hope by the power of the Holy Spirit that abides in us. We are grateful. Blessings

177

Good Morning!

The Lord is my strength and my shield; My heart trusted in Him, and I am helped; Therefore my heart greatly rejoices, And with my song I will praise Him. **Psalm 28:7 NKJV**

The Lord enables him to be strong in the face of the enemy's oppression. A shield not only provides a warrior with physical protection it also serves to boost the warrior's confidence. Experienced believers can often recall many occasions when the Lord strengthened and protected us. Every victory brings an opportunity to rejoice and be thankful. We honor You Lord for the opportunity to worship You. Blessings

178

Good Morning!

Stand fast therefore in the liberty by which Christ has made us free, and do not be entangled again with a yoke of bondage.
Galatians 5:1 NKJV

Paul is speaking about rebellion against sin and slavery. He told the Galatians and, by extension, all Christians that Christ has set us free, so we ought to stand firm. We should not take that yoke of slavery again. In other words, believers ought not let anyone tell them they must follow all of the rules and restrictions of the law of Moses to be right with God. All glory to God for His Grace and His faithfulness. Amen. Blessings

179

Good Morning!

Glory in His holy name; Let the hearts of those rejoice who seek the Lord!
1 Chronicles 16:10 NKJV

Those of us who give glory to God's name are allowed to glory in it. We value ourselves based on our relation to Him and face each day based on His promises to us. Let the heart of those who rejoice seek the Lord, much more than those who have found Him. There is strength in seeking Him. Blessings

180

Good Morning!

Serve the Lord with gladness;
Come before His presence with singing.
Psalm 100:2 NKJV

This calls upon those of us who read or hear song of Zion to serve God with a sense of joy. The imagery of someone singing suggests intense happiness, it's such an appropriate feeling when we truly understand what God has done for us. We are eternally grateful. Blessings

181

Good Morning!

Therefore the Lord Himself will give you a sign: Behold, the virgin shall conceive and bear a Son, and shall call His name Immanuel. **Isaiah 7:14 NKJV**

Isaiah foretells that the promised Messiah, Jesus, will be born of Mary, who will conceive without the involvement of any human father. Thank you on this day for reminding us that God is with us and that we shouldn't fear what any person may do to us. Let's not look to ourselves for deliverance but rather trust in the baby born of a virgin in Bethlehem because the Lord is with Him and He will be with all who trust in Him. We are so grateful to God for our Savior. Blessings

182

Good Morning!

Then King David sent and brought him out of the house of Machir the son of Ammiel, from Lo Debar.
2 Samuel 9:5 NKJV

Lo Debar, was a place of desolation, isolation and separation from God. Mephibosheth was in London Debar. David made a promise with Jonathan to protect his family. David showed grace to Mephibosheth because of Jonathan's worth and faithfulness. David offered to take all the blessings, honor and acceptance earned by Jonathan and shower them on his son, Mephibosheth. This crippled man was blessed because of the faithfulness of his father. Who will receive blessings and honor because of your faithfulness? Blessings

183

Good Morning!

Then these men were bound in their coats, their trousers, their turbans, and their other garments, and were cast into the midst of the burning fiery furnace. 22 Therefore, because the king's command was urgent, and the furnace exceedingly hot, the flame of the fire killed those men who took up Shadrach, Meshach, and Abed-Nego. 23 And these three men, Shadrach, Meshach, and Abed-Nego, fell down bound into the midst of the burning fiery furnace.
Daniel 3:21-22 NKJV

No man is strong enough to resist judgment by the One True God, whom these Hebrew men worshiped. Someday, all nations of the world will attempt a military coup against God but they will not be able to withstand His judgement. As kings of the earth set themselves apart, and the rulers take counsel together, against and against His Anointed, our God will speak to them in His wrath, and terrify them in His fury. Who can stand against Him? Blessings

184

Good Morning!

And she will bring forth a Son, and you shall call His name Jesus, for He will save His people from their sins. **Matthew 1:21 NKJV**

Before Joseph could end the relationship with Mary, an angel from God appeared to Joseph in a dream.
The angel tells Joseph not to fear going through with the marriage. Mary is pregnant by the Holy Spirit, not by sexual sin, and not from another man. The angel continues in this verse with more details. The baby is a boy. You will call His name Jesus, because He will save His people from their sins. We are so thankful and so grateful to God for our Savior. All glory to the Most High God for His faithfulness.
Blessings

185 Good Morning!

He who has pity on the poor lends to the Lord, And He will pay back what he has given. **Psalm 19:17 NKJV**

When we are kind and generous to those who are incapable of repaying us, we are actually being kind and generous to the Lord Charity honors God, and a person who helps the needy does God's will as well as God's work. The implication of the term lend suggests that God will repay those who are generous, not necessarily with earthly wealth, but in spiritual blessing. Thank You Lord. We are grateful. Blessings

186

Good Morning!

My flesh and my heart fail;
But God is the strength of my
heart and my portion forever.
Psalm 73:26. NKJV

This verse teaches us that we shouldn't rely on our own strength because it will fail us. Instead we should look to God and rely on his strength. We are capable of making mistakes. The premise of this psalm is that we should not become bitter and unhappy when we don't understand God's ways. God as the most important aspect of our lives. Even if our health fails or our circumstances become dire, we know in the midst of it all, God can never fail us. We are forever grateful. Blessings

187

Good Morning!

Therefore, as we have opportunity, let us do good to all, especially to those who are of the household of faith.
Galatians 6:10 NKJV

Paul has urged the Galatian Christians not to grow tired of doing good, through the power of God's Spirit. God has a reward for Christians who serve Him well in giving to those in need. The foundation of Christianity was built on the principle of bringing all to the church and having it distributed evenly so that no one would lack. So let's all strive to be intentional about doing good to and for other believers. God is pleased with the cheerful giver who has an humble heart. Blessings

188

Good Morning!

He gives power to the weak,
And to those who have no might
He increases strength.
Isaiah 40:29 NKJV

Our God is not only the sovereign, inexhaustible, creator of all things, His knowledge has no end and He is always giving and compassionate with us. He is willing to bend down and provide for our needs. But, such grace requires patience from us. Thank you Lord for being the power we need in our weak moments and the strength we desire when our energy dwindles, we are eternally grateful. Blessings

189

Good Morning!

The Lord has established His throne in heaven, And His kingdom rules over all.
Psalm 103:19 NKJV

In this verse David declares God's sovereignty. Our Lord has prepared His throne in the heavens and His rule extends to everyone and everything. Lucifer, the Devil, tried and failed to remove the Lord from His throne (Isaiah 14:12–15). Throughout history and even today evil men have followed in Lucifer's footsteps, but they continue to learn the hard way that our Lord is sovereign and invincible. All glory to our Most High God, His throne is firmly fixed. Amen. Blessings

190

Good Morning!

He has made everything beautiful in its time. Also He has put eternity in their hearts, except that no one can find out the work that God does from beginning to end.
Ecclesiastes 3:11 NKJV

When we walk through challenges and we don't understand why things are happening or where something is going, to know that God sees it all, that He knows it all, that He sees things we don't see regarding what has led to this point and what will come from this point, reminds us that the struggles and toils we experience in this world, will not have the last word. We trust in the God who sees all time, and sees our circumstances in the context of all eternity. God has put in all of us a sense that this world is not all there is, that there is more beyond what we see, both in the past and in the present. Let's strive to continue to trust God to help us to live each day without being consumed by what may happen next. Thank you Lord. Blessings

191

Good Morning!

In the beginning God created the heavens and the earth.
Genesis 1:1 NKJV

God wants us to see Him first and foremost as the Creator. Of course, everyone won't agree that the Bible is the authoritative and inspired Word of God. But what's beyond debate is that the opening words of the Bible clearly claim that God, whom we have come to know as the God of Israel, created the heavens and the earth. He created everything in the natural world from the heavens, the sky, and space, to our planet and everything on it. Who is bold enough to refuse to serve a God as powerful and influential as this? Blessings

Good Morning!

192

But be doers of the word, and not hearers only, deceiving yourselves. 23 For if anyone is a hearer of the word and not a doer, he is like a man observing his natural face in a mirror; 24 for he observes himself, goes away, and immediately forgets what kind of man he was. **James 1:22-23 NKJV**

We go to the house of worship or other places where the word is spoken, we are emotionally moved, we agree with what we hear, shout amen, and praise the hearing of the truth. But as soon as we depart the place, the word that moved us to a seemingly higher place in God, actually never entered our spirit, so it's left in the fabric of the atmosphere. We forget the word, we never gain or retain the knowledge and power that the word can bring, it's like looking in the mirror at the wretched broken people we are, we dislike that individual whom we have grown into so we forget what we really look like as soon as we step away from the mirror. Let's strive to imitate the Lord more, study and soak up His word, meditate on it, so when we hear or read the word it will be sown into the fabric of our being and we will see God in the mirror of every aspect of our lives daily. Blessings

193

Good Morning!

Your word I have hidden in my heart,
That I might not sin against You.
Psalm 119:11 NKJV

The word of God is a powerful antidote against sin, when it has a place in our heart; not only the precepts of it forbid sin, but as we internalize it, the power of it helps us to repel sin. The word of Christ should dwell richly in us. If God's word is only in the Bible, and not in our heart, we may soon and easily be lured back into our sinful ways. Thank you Lord for giving us an opportunity to study Your word, meditate on it, and hide it in our hearts. Blessings

194

Good Morning!

Teach me to do Your will, For You are my God; Your Spirit is good. Lead me in the land of uprightness.
Psalm 143:10 NKJV

Our hearts cry out to God asking Him to teach us to do His will and for the Spirit to guide us to the place where we can walk on solid ground and live the life that pleases God. Rather than giving up when things seem to be too much for us, we cry out to our Father in heaven and trust that the Holy Spirit will bring His answer and His power into our lives along with God's favor and His deliverance. We are grateful. Blessings

195

Good Morning!

And do not be conformed to this world, but be transformed by the renewing of your mind, that you may prove what is that good and acceptable and perfect will of God. **Romans 12:2 NKJV**

This scripture teaches us that we can live out God's will when we change our thoughts to His thoughts, rather than living as the world wants us to live. When we strive to live for God, this scripture teaches us how we can faithfully follow Him and discover the peace and joy He has for us. Thank you Lord for giving us the strength to renew our mind daily so that we may prove and do Your will for our lives. We are grateful. Amen. Blessings

196

Good Morning!

Arise, shine; For your light has come! And the glory of the Lord is risen upon you. **Isaiah 60:1 NKJV**

The world has been plunged into darkness, but our Lord releases divine light to all people. Those whom He has chosen need to always strive to be a lantern of brightness and strength to guide others to our Savior. As we allow our divine light to flow over others, the smallest will become a class of elite individuals and the least will become a mighty nation. Peace, prestige, and power is our destiny. We are so thankful for His light and His powerful word. Blessings

197

Good Morning!

And let us consider one another in order to stir up love and good works, 25 not forsaking the assembling of ourselves together, as is the manner of some, but exhorting one another, and so much the more as you see the Day approaching.
Hebrews 10:24-25 NKJV

Our purpose as believers is to stir up and stimulate other Christians to love and good works. The spiritual reality and need for us to assemble in the sanctuary is more than an official meeting. It's a call to be empowered by God and do life better together. Forsaking fellowship allows for discouragement, doubt, and depression. These multiply in isolation. When there is no fellowship, there is no stirring of love or any opportunities to exhort one another. Lord thank you for teaching us to assemble to support and encourage one another. Blessings

198

Good Morning!

Do not remember the former things, Nor consider the things of old. 19 Behold, I will do a new thing, Now it shall spring forth; Shall you not know it? I will even make a road in the wilderness And rivers in the desert.
Isaiah 43:18-19 NKJV

Our God loves doing new things. He makes paths through the wilderness just for us. Our future deliverance will surpass the former deliverance of the Israelites from Egyptian bondage in unparalleled splendor and glory. A new creation, a new heaven and a new earth, are promised in the word of God, a place free from sin or defilement. When Moses struck the rock, rather than speak to it as he was told, God still allowed an abundance of water to flow from the rock so that the people and their animals could drink in the desert. Our life before Christ was aimless, as we wandered without hope or purpose. Let's not fixate so much on the wilderness of this life that we forget about what's ahead, eternal life that He promised after this. Blessings

199 *Good Morning!*

A friend loves at all times,
And a brother is born for adversity.
Proverbs 17:17 NKJV

Ruth was a true friend to Naomi. She showed the epitome of friendship when she said to Naomi, "wherever you go, I will go; And wherever you lodge, I will lodge; Your people shall be my people, And your God, my God." (Ruth 1:16). The meaning is that being willing to meet another person's need is a sign of true friendship. False and shallow companions don't act like friends, at all, when the relationship might cost them something. We must consistently strive to show ourselves friendly because a true friend is always loving, and helpful in trying times. A true friend and always exhibits true love in unfavorable circumstances as well as in favorable ones. Lord we thank you and praise you for the true friends in our lives. Blessings

200

Good Morning!

Therefore, we do not lose heart. Even though our outward man is perishing, yet the inward man is being renewed day by day. **2 Corinthians 4:16 NKJV**

Our God will use fragile vessels to carry His powerful truth. When we refuse to lose heart, meaning we will not give in to the temptation to live in despair and desperation, God keeps us safe. At times, our outward appearance can be deceiving. We may look exhausted and frustrated because of our daily tests and trials. But what the world can't see is our inner man, who renews our strength and makes us new daily. The inner man reminds us that we are equipped with strength and determination to run on and fulfill our purpose which is to carry the light of the gospel to the world. We are grateful for the strength to keep moving even when we don't feel like running to do His will. Blessings

201

Good Morning!

One thing I have desired of the Lord, That will I seek: That I may dwell in the house of the Lord All the days of my life,
To behold the beauty of the Lord, And to inquire in His temple. **Psalm 27:4 NKJV**

Sometimes trouble drives us closer to the Lord and makes us more desirous of worshiping Him in the fellowship of other believers. When you find yourself in the wilderness seeking refuge from your enemies, your heart should be in the tabernacle seeking the beauty of God. Our ultimate goal is to spend eternity in worship to our Lord. Amen. Blessings

202

Good Morning!

Fear not, for I am with you; Be not dismayed, for I am your God. I will strengthen you, Yes, I will help you, I will uphold you with My righteous right hand. **Isaiah 41:10 NKJV**

God has promised to be with us at all times, God has a covenantal commitment to Abraham and all of His descendants to never leave us. He doesn't want us to fear or be apprehensive about our future or what may happen today. He will strengthen and help us to overcome every thing that overwhelms us. When we find ourselves in a position where there is nothing but opposition, seek His help and His righteous hand, He will reveal the purpose for that season. Stand on His word, be still and know that He is God and He's always present with us. We are grateful. Blessings

203

Good Morning!

God is our refuge and strength,
A very present help in trouble
Psalm 46:1 NKJV

This psalm reflects on God's miraculous deliverance of His people but doesn't specify an exact event. There are many possibilities, one of which is when the Assyrians laid siege to Jerusalem and advised King Hezekiah to surrender. Hezekiah prayed, and God answered. In God we find salvation and glory, He is our rock and the strength of our lives. We can trust in Him at all times. In God, we have someone we can pour our heart out to and trust in Him for guidance and direction. He's always present and when life threatens to overwhelm us, He will hide us in the shadows of His strength and power until we are strong enough to face another day. We are eternally grateful. Blessings

204

Good Morning!

Behold, God is my salvation, I will trust and not be afraid; 'For Yah, the Lord, is my strength and song; He also has become my salvation.'
Isaiah 12:2 NKJV

Isaiah is delivering a promise to God's people. The day will come when the offspring of Jesse, Jesus the Son of God, will establish His kingdom on earth from His throne in Jerusalem. God's people will sing the words God has wanted to hear from us all along. We will sing that God is our salvation and our source of trust. We won't need to be afraid, the Lord is our source of stability, safety, and power. These words have always been true for those who belong to God. However, many have proven time and again that they do not believe them. Do you believe? Blessings

205

Good Morning!

Depart from evil and do good;
Seek peace and pursue it.
Psalm 34:14 NKJV

David reminds us how important it is to reject temptation, whether it comes from evildoers or from our own evil nature. Instead of doing wrong, we should do what is good and seek to live a peaceful life. We need to pursue peace, we ought to strive for it, to try hard to obtain it. Making peace manifests a God fearing attitude James 3:18. Thank You Lord for an attitude that shows your goodness as we are directed away from evil. We are so grateful. Blessings

206

Good Morning!

And you will seek Me and find Me, when you search for Me with all your heart.
Jeremiah 29:13 NKJV

In order to really find God, this verse is saying that we must seek Him with all of our hearts. We can't casually try to seek God a little here and there and expect to really find Him. We must dive in and seek Him with everything we have in order to really find Him and get to know Him. As we put God first and seek Him, He will restore all that has been taken, all that we have allowed to be taken, and all that we gave away because we didn't think we were worthy. Thank you Lord for teaching us to seek You with our whole heart daily. We are grateful. Blessings

207

Good Morning!

Therefore know that the Lord your God, He is God, the faithful God who keeps covenant and mercy for a thousand generations with those who love Him and keep His commandments
Deuteronomy 7:9 NKJV

Our Lord is faithful, He keeps us from all evil. His promises are true. When we are faithless, He remains faithful because He can't deny Himself. Even when we are too weak to have any faith left. When we choose to trust in ourselves, or in our job, or in our bank account, He remains faithful. He will not disown anyone who has accepted Him. He will surely carry out His promises to the end. Let's vow to petition our Lord for the restoration of our nation, by praying for the depravity of man and the merciful nature of God because the healing of our land is based on God's mercies and His covenantal faithfulness. We are so thankful and so grateful for the promises of our God. Blessings

208

Good Morning!

But this I say: He who sows sparingly will also reap sparingly, and he who sows bountifully will also reap bountifully.
2 Corinthians 9:6 NKJV

Our financial contributions to the needs of other believers can bring spiritual results. The more we can plant out of a heart of true, Christlike love for our spiritual siblings, the more love our spiritual crops will bear. These results are not in money coming back to the us, it's in the spiritual lives of the givers and those who receive our gifts. In this sense, money becomes more than just money. It becomes evidence of love given in the name of Christ. Lord help us to always strive to sow bountifully to the things of the Spirit. Blessings

209

Good Morning!

Sow for yourselves righteousness; Reap in mercy; Break up your fallow ground, For it is time to seek the Lord, Till He comes and rains righteousness on you. **Hosea 10:12 NKJV**

This is a call to righteousness, it's a call to bold, complete, tender forgiveness. In some ways it's simple to accept but seeing it through, as in any relationship takes a concerted effort even in those seasons of emptiness. Seeking and serving God requires deep rooted determination not fair weather, faithfulness. When a farmer sows seed, they are looking to harvest what is planted. When a farmer is reaping, they do so faithfully because of what was sown. God is calling for the same kind of deep hearted efforts when we follow Him. He looks beyond the outward show of remorse, He wants us to dedicate ourselves to a deep inner, sustained, gesture of commitment. We are to sow with a view to righteousness and reap in mercy and loving kindness, this sowing is rooted in loyalty and trust. We are so grateful for the opportunity to sow to righteousness. Blessings

210

Good Morning!

So then neither he who plants is anything,
nor he who waters,
but God who gives the increase.
1 Corinthians 3:7 NKJV

Growing the church is like farming, we need plants and the plants need water. Neither one as a sole entity makes the plant grow, both planting and watering are required for ministry growth. But all the human contribution in the world is still not sufficient for the plant to grow, plants need God's sovereign intervention. Neither the one who plants nor the one who waters have any real power. The field hand doesn't do magic, he does his assigned job. That work matters, but the work in and of itself cannot make seeds grow. Only God can give growth to the seed. That's real power. God, then, is the only one worth following. We are grateful for a God worth following. Blessings

211

Good Morning!

Therefore be patient, brethren, until the coming of the Lord. See how the farmer waits for the precious fruit of the earth, waiting patiently for it until it receives the early and latter rain. 8 You also be patient. Establish your hearts, for the coming of the Lord is at hand. **James 5:7-8 NKJV**

Waiting is hard when we're suffering. James uses the analogy of a farmer for encouragement. He asks us to think of how hardworking farm hands have to wait for the payoff of their efforts. The reality of God's promise, His pledge to rescue us and make things right, gives us the ability to stand strong, even when our circumstances threaten to overwhelm us. We must stand still and wait for the salvation of our Lord. Blessings

212

Good Morning!

Then He said to His disciples, "The harvest truly is plentiful, but the laborers are few. ³⁸ Therefore pray the Lord of the harvest to send out laborers into His harvest."
Matthew 9:37-38 NKJV

Jesus seems to be saying that many people are ready to believe in Jesus and be welcomed into the kingdom of heaven. Jesus understands that this is our greatest need. This is how we will be rescued from our harassed and helpless condition and given peace, joy, and the hope of an eternal home with our Father. There's a place for all believers to serve in the kingdom. We can pray earnestly and go out as a laborer of the gospel. Jesus identifies two roles that believers can fill on this side: pray continuously and go out as laborers to spread the gospel to all who will hear. Do your part. Blessings

213

Good Morning!

In this manner, therefore, pray: Our Father in heaven, Hallowed be Your name. [10] Your kingdom come, Your will be done On earth as it is in heaven. [11] Give us this day our daily bread. [12] And forgive us our debts, As we forgive our debtors. [13] And do not lead us into temptation, But deliver us from the evil one. For Yours is the kingdom and the power and the glory forever.
Matthew 9:9-13 NKJV

Thank you Lord for this prayer of strength and sustainment for our time of need. We are forever grateful. Blessings

214 Good Morning!

Now this is the confidence that we have in Him, that if we ask anything according to His will, He hears us.
1 John 5:13 NKJV

We must have a relationship with God before we go to Him seeking an answer to our prayers because getting a positive answer to prayer is based on asking "according to His will." We should have confidence in our prayers. As believers we know we will have eternal life and our faithful God continues to hear and answer our prayers. We are forever grateful. Blessings

215

Good Morning!

Be anxious for nothing, but in everything by prayer and supplication, with thanksgiving, let your requests be made known to God; 7 and the peace of God, which surpasses all understanding, will guard your hearts and minds through Christ Jesus. **Philippians 4:6-7 NKJV**

Even in the vibrant, dynamic first century church, petty quarrels were threatening to disrupt fellowship. Paul begged these women by name to stop their strife and let their true companion, the Holy Ghost, to help them overcome the division among them. He focused their minds on all that they had to be thankful for in Christ Jesus so they could lift their eyes from their mind-dividing, fellowship-splitting strife up to the peace and joy found only in Jesus. The peace which comes only from God will stand guard over the believers' hearts and minds by means of Jesus Christ. We must strive to not be anxious, divided, or distracted over nothing. Let's give wings to anxiety and every paralyzing worry, turn it into prayer, anticipating, even while we are asking, a loving God's reply with thanksgiving. Be encouraged. Blessings

216

Good Morning!

Now the Lord came and stood and called as at other times, "Samuel! Samuel!" And Samuel answered, "Speak, for Your servant hears." **1 Samuel 3:10 NKJV**

The back-and-forth game of running to Eli after hearing his name called is over. Eli recognized that it was the Lord calling young Samuel and told Samuel how to respond if it happened again. Maybe the Lord allowed Samuel to run to Eli those three times to confirm, for both of them, that the Lord had really communicated with Samuel. Before we go, let's strive to make sure God has called our name. We don't want to move in any direction that God has not predestined and preordained just for us. Blessings

217

Good Morning!

Likewise the Spirit also helps in our weaknesses. For we do not know what we should pray for as we ought, but the Spirit Himself makes intercession for us with groanings which cannot be uttered.
Romans 8:26 NKJV

The Holy Spirit is present within us to assist us with moments of moral, physical, or emotional weakness. Sometimes we confront difficulties so insurmountable we can't put any words of prayer together. We know we need to approach God, but we feel as if we have said all that we know to say to Him. In these instances, the promise is that the Holy Spirit makes intercession for us with groanings that cannot be uttered. During these times, we aren't speaking at all, our communication with God is through the Holy Spirit and it is all nonverbal. Thank You Lord for the Holy Spirit that speaks on our behalf when we are unable to form a thought for prayer. Amen. Blessings

218

Good Morning!

Then He spoke a parable to them, that men always ought to pray and not lose heart. **Luke 18:1 NKJV**

Jesus has just explained to the disciples what the world will look like when He returns. People will not be thinking about God. They will be living their normal lives, marrying, working, and planning. Like the people of the days of Noah and Lot, they won't realize that judgment is imminent. When Jesus comes, He will separate His followers from those who reject Him. Even the closest relationships will be broken. Lord, thank you for the time to prepare for Your return. Let's use it wisely. Blessings

219

Good Morning!

Judge not, that you be not judged. 2 For with what judgment you judge, you will be judged; and with the measure you use, it will be measured back to you.
Matthew 7:1-2 NKJV

Let's not judge others until we are prepared to be judged by the same standard. And then, when we exercise judgment toward others, let's do it with humility and always under the guidance of the Holy Spirit. We are grateful. Blessings

220

Good Morning!

Take heed, watch and pray;
for you do not know when the time is.
Mark 13:33 NKJV

Jesus isn't saying that we should spend all our time and effort in determining when He will return because no man knows the day nor the hour. He is warning that there is no time for leisurely faith. So, we should walk carefully, not as the unwise but as the wise believer, making the best use of the time we have because the days are numbered and at times, filled with turmoil. Let's strive to stay awake and pray that we may have strength to escape all the things that are not of God so when our time comes we can give account of our actions and reactions in this life. Let's be watchful and prayerful as we wait for His return. Blessings

221

Good Morning!

I will instruct you and teach you in the way you should go; I will guide you with My eye. **Psalm 32:8 NKJV**

Spending time with God helps us to get to know Him better and be ready to hear what He has to say concerning our future. God knows us better than anyone. We are honored and forever grateful for His guidance. Blessings

222 *Good Morning!*

casting down arguments and every high thing that exalts itself against the knowledge of God, bringing every thought into captivity to the obedience of Christ. **2 Corinthians 10:5 NKJV**

In this scripture, the Corinthians were attempting to undermine Paul's authority as an apostle. The battlefield in question is not an earthly region, but the hearts and minds of the people in Corinth. In God's power, Paul and his co-workers for Christ were able to destroy all the arguments and impressive-sounding opinions his opponents put forward against the knowledge of God. Using godly tools, Paul and his associates destroyed the feeble arguments of the Corinthians, and motivated them to obey Christ. Lord we are so thankful and so grateful for the sound lessons that we have available to us in Your word. Amen. Blessings

223

Good Morning!

Through the Lord's mercies we are not consumed, Because His compassions fail not. 23 They are new every morning; Great is Your faithfulness.
Lamentations 3:22-23 NKJV

No matter what we have done, or wherever we have been, God's mercies are new for us every morning. His steadfast love will never fail us. He's made a way for us to get back to Him and live in the love, joy, and peace that He has for us. This scripture is a powerful reminder of what God has done for us. And it's a verse that each of us should reflect on and commit to memory for those times when we find ourselves overwhelmed with the tests and trials of life. Lord we honor and glorify You for Your word that soothes our soul during our time of stress and frustration. We are grateful. Blessings

224

Good Morning!

And He said to them, Go into all the world and preach the gospel to every creature.
Mark 16:15 NKJV

Just like the disciples, we have been commissioned with a worldwide missionary assignment to spread the gospel to the whole world. Christ's Resurrection broke the power of sin and death in the lives of all who choose to place their trust in Him, so Christ's commission remains the same today. As long as He keeps waking us up, we have much work to do. Blessings

225

Good Morning!

as His divine power has given to us all things that pertain to life and godliness, through the knowledge of Him who called us by glory and virtue,
2 Peter 1:3 NKJV

This Scripture is reminding us that all we need in this life, God has already given us. We are prepared for anything. All the opportunities we will have, information that we will ever need, and every relationship that we will become involved in has already been given to us through knowing Him. In all these things, He wants us to have peace so let's strive to seek Him first so that He can perfect the work He has begun in us. Be encouraged. Blessings

226

Good Morning!

Let this mind be in you which was also in Christ Jesus
Philippians 2:5 NKJV

In our relationships with one another, we should have the same mindset as Christ Jesus. With a desire to accurately represent our Lord, Paul urged His followers to reflect the humility, self-sacrifice, and compassion of Jesus for others. Thank you Lord for teaching us to strive to have our minds set on those things above. We are grateful. Blessings

227

Good Morning!

Oh, taste and see that the Lord is good;
Blessed is the man who trusts in Him!
Psalm 34:8 NKJV

This verse reminds us that God is our shelter from the storms of life He protects us from danger that seeks to hurt us physically, from distress that overwhelms us emotionally, and from different circumstances that attempt to destroy us spiritually. Let's strive to feed on the Lord and accept His truth deep into our hearts each day. This requires us to read the written Word of God out of obedience to His will. Blessings

228

Good Morning!

And we urge you, brethren, to recognize those who labor among you, and are over you in the Lord and admonish you, 13. and to esteem them very highly in love for their work's sake. Be at peace among yourselves. **1 Thessalonians 5:12-13 NKJV**

The spiritual leaders whom God has appointed over us are those who labor among us. We are to project an attitude of respect and love towards pastors and those whom God has placed over us. Also the congregation is warned, to know those who labor among us, which indicates a closeness of fellowship. Negativity and dissension has no place in the church. If we live love and peace daily, unity will abide amongst us all in the building. Are you projecting an aura of unity daily? Blessings

229

Good Morning!

I will praise You, O Lord, with my whole heart; I will tell of all Your marvelous works.
Psalm 9:1 NKJV

When we hear this command to give thanks in all things and we think about the difficult circumstances that we have been called to go through, it may seem difficult to be thankful in all things. Yes, we have been wronged in one way or another. How do we give thanks in the middle of those circumstances? Obviously, we're not thankful for evil, for being wronged, but we are thankful for God's sovereignty over these things. We're thankful because we have Him beside us at all times, we can rejoice because we are never alone, so yes, we will praise Him because regardless of what we are going through, He is always faithful. We are grateful. Blessings

230

Good Morning!

And above all things have fervent love for one another, for love will cover a multitude of sins.
1 Peter 4:8 NKJV

Regardless of what we go through, we need to show love to one another. We are Christ representatives, the essence of God is love so we should strive to love, respect, and forgive without limit as we follow the example of our Savior. When we allow love to be the dominant theme in all our lives, we can experience the amazing grace and perfect peace that comes when our sins are covered. With the love of Christ in our heart, we will know the liberating joy that floods our soul when our sins are covered by Christ our Savior, the lover of our soul. We are grateful. Blessings

231

Good Morning!

For whoever desires to save his life will lose it, but whoever loses his life for My sake and the gospel will save it.
Mark 8:35 NKJV

This verse does not demand martyrdom in order to secure life. However, the passage does establish that all who come to Christ must give Him their lives in such totality that we retain no claim on it. Having placed ourselves forever in the hands of Christ, we immediately possess abundant life. Life is found in living for Jesus. Anything else is lost in death, so let's passionately pursue Jesus and life in Him. Thank you Lord for abundant life. Amen. Blessings

232

Good Morning!

The Gentiles shall come to your light,
And kings to the brightness of your rising.
Isaiah 60:3 NKJV

Israel received the perfect light of the Lord, the light of salvation to the nations. They were assured that even in the midst of great darkness the Lord will arise even as the sun comes up in Zion. This entire chapter was addressed to Israel over 2000 years ago. The command to arise is accompanied by the strength of the Lord to fulfill that directive. In light of all that is happening in Israel on this day, we are assured that the gospel will continue to shine so bright that well-disposed heathens will not only congratulate those who profess the gospel and wish them much joy, but they will rejoice to participate with them in their happiness. Our God is still faithful, He is still God, His promises are still true, in the midst of the struggles that have to be endured in this world, we will operate in the strength of our Lord. Amen. Blessings

233

Good Morning!

Now no chastening seems to be joyful for the present, but painful; nevertheless, afterward it yields the peaceable fruit of righteousness to those who have been trained by it. **Hebrews 12:11 NKJV**

Rather than a painful promise, these verses present the basis for happy optimism for all Christians. The strongest evidence of spiritual sonship can be deduced from the intervention of God in the life of the believer for chastisement. God's discipline yields the peaceable fruit of righteousness in the lives of His children, and it is for our profit. These acts of God are evidence of His love. Lord we thank You for chastening us in love, it keeps us on the path of righteousness. Glory. Amen. Blessings

234

Good Morning!

The heavens declare the glory of God; And the firmament shows His handiwork. **Psalms 19:1 NKJV**

This psalm illustrates the two general categories of revelation, natural revelation-God's revelation of Himself through the created order and special revelation- God's revealing of Himself through the scriptures. Science continues to deepen our appreciation for God's design. The more we learn about how the universe is structured, and how it works, the more fully we can grasp the power of God. The natural world reveals that God is wise, powerful, and eternal. He is my eternal God. Please understand that God's revelation of Himself in nature leaves those who reject Him without excuse. All will stand before Him and give an account of our actions and choices in this life. Choose wisely. Blessings

235

Good Morning!

So shall My word be that goes forth from My mouth; It shall not return to Me void, But it shall accomplish what I please, And it shall prosper in the thing for which I sent it.
Isaiah 55:11 NKJV

People will say things they don't mean. They will make commitments and not follow through, but our God is the exact opposite, He keeps every promise He has made. If God has spoken it, He will make it happen. His words aren't empty and mindless and no word He has spoken will return null, void or empty It is the divine origin (or character) of God's word, and not some magical power which causes it to accomplish the purpose for which it is sent. Thank You Lord for the faithfulness behind every word that You have spoken. Blessings

236

Good Morning!

Enter by the narrow gate; for wide is the gate and broad is the way that leads to destruction, and there are many who go in by it. [14]Because narrow is the gate and difficult is the way which leads to life, and there are few who find it.
Matthew 7:13-14 NKJV

The way of life in the kingdom is the way of profession in practice, how are we living? The urgency and sternness of these verses mark the sermon as more than an ethical issue. These verses constitute an appeal for a decision. Popular religious contemplation imagines that almost all will eventually be saved, but Jesus suggests the opposite. Only a few, relatively speaking, will be saved. Will you find the way? Blessings

237

Good Morning!

And God is able to make all grace abound toward you, that you, always having all sufficiency in all things, may have an abundance for every good work.
2 Corinthians 9:8 NKJV

God increases the ability of believers who give generously to give even more. This results in increasing His righteousness on earth, as well as in causing thankfulness to Him for overflow. He will be glorified by those who receive the gift and pray for those who give. Giving for Christians is an act of faith, trusting God to meet our needs while becoming the method by which He meets the needs of others. Thank you Lord for blessing us with more than enough to accomplish all the good works you want to see from us. We are grateful. Blessings

238 Good Morning!

Seek the Lord and His strength;
Seek His face evermore!
1 Chronicles 16:11 NKJV

This scripture tells us to search for the Lord and His strength and to seek His face always. In a world full of sin and brokenness, the only place to find strength is in our relationship with Him. Our security is in the sacrificial death, burial, and resurrection of Jesus. In spite of the sorrow, pandemics, murders, and tragedies in this world, He is always available to us, we can seek His strength and meditate on His face because He is our refuge. Amen. Blessings

239

Good Morning!

For the mountains shall depart
And the hills be removed, But My kindness shall not depart from you,
Nor shall My covenant of peace be removed, Says the Lord, who has mercy on you. **Isaiah 54:10 NKJV**

When troubles on earth seem to prevail, there is something to be said about committing it all to our Savior. He will give us a peace that is far beyond any comfort we can find in this world. We are so thankful and so grateful that our Lord, will have mercy on us. Blessings

240

Good Morning!

Ask, and it will be given to you; seek, and you will find; knock, and it will be opened to you. **Matthew 7:7 NKJV**

This verse describes God as a generous Father who is eager to give good gifts to His praying children. Don't stop asking, even when it seems like He isn't going to answer, don't stop seeking because He promised us we would find what we need in Him, don't stop knocking with patient endurance and steadfast perseverance. We are to knock with confidence and humility even when life's circumstances seem to test our faith and sap our strength. Keep praying, it works. Blessings

241

Good Morning!

A friend loves at all times,
And a brother is born for adversity.
Proverbs 17:17 NKJV

Solomon points out the value of a true friend and a brother. He says a true friend is always loving, and a brother helps in trying times. A true friend and genuine brother exhibit true love in unfavorable circumstances as well as the favorable ones. A true friend or brother draws alongside a hurting person when that person experiences sickness or pain or financial distress or the loss of a loved one. The genuine and compassionate friend or brother is sure to stand with you through it all. Amen. Blessings

242

Good Morning!

And now, Lord, what do I wait for?
My hope is in You.
Psalm 39:7 NKJV

Life is incredibly short. All of our human effort is nothing compared to the power of our God. As you scrabble to acquire earthly things, know that all of your scrabbling is in vain. Lord thank you for reminding us that all of our hope is in You. Amen. Blessings

243

Good Morning!

Your kingdom come.
Your will be done On earth as it is in heaven. **Matthew 6:10 NKJV**

God works all things according to the counsel of His will. God is sovereign and that means His plans always prevail. The fact that He is a supreme being is best represented on the cross. Lord, we honor you for reminding us to seek You and pray for Your will to be done in our lives at all times. We are grateful. Blessings

244

Good Morning!

And Jesus went about all Galilee, teaching in their synagogues, preaching the gospel of the kingdom, and healing all kinds of sickness and all kinds of disease among the people. **Matthew 4:23 NKJV**

It was common for worship in the synagogue to include preaching from various rabbis who wished to speak. Jesus and His disciples traveled from place to place, likely keeping an exhausting schedule. Jesus' message everywhere He went was the "gospel of the kingdom." He verified His claim to be the Messiah by supernaturally meeting the needs of the people. This included miraculously healing all kinds of diseases and different afflictions. These blessings of healing and relief from suffering showed that Jesus really was the Ruler of the kingdom of heaven. We are grateful for our Healer, Ruler, and King of glory. Blessings

245

Good Morning!

Blow the trumpet in Zion, And sound an alarm in My holy mountain! Let all the inhabitants of the land tremble; For the day of the Lord is coming, For it is at hand
Joel 2:1 NKJV

This verse gives us a graphic and descriptive precursor of the terrible time that is yet to come. We see the signs daily. The trumpet call was the wake-up call for Israel to prepare for a battle and Joel urges God's people: "Blow a shofar in Zion. Sound an alarm on My holy mountain! Let all the inhabitants of the land tremble, for the day of the LORD is coming surely it is near." These urgent words of warning come from the Lord Himself and emphasized that the great and dreadful 'Day of the Lord' is close at hand. There is no time to delay. We must choose a side, the time is now. Thank you Lord for reminding us to be vigilant and diligent for You. Blessings

246

Good Morning!

But the Helper, the Holy Spirit, whom the Father will send in My name, He will teach you all things, and bring to your remembrance all things that I said to you. **John 14:26 NKJV**

He recognized the necessity for a comforter, a teacher, someone who stands beside us at all times, still teaching us and reminding us of His ways and His heart for the world. It is grace to us that Jesus, our priest, savior, and teacher came to us, but did not leave us to ourselves. Jesus knew that the Holy Spirit would be exactly what we would need. This is grace to us and we are forever grateful. Amen. Blessings

247

Good Morning!

Blessed be the God and Father of our Lord Jesus Christ, who according to His abundant mercy has begotten us again to a living hope through the resurrection of Jesus Christ from the dead. **1 Peter 1:3 NKJV**

It's one thing to hope we will be saved, to yearn for life after death. Jesus proved that this hope is not a fantasy. He died, then showed Himself alive to many witnesses. Our faith is not a wish for a better world. The reason for our hope in an eternity with the Father is that our Lord is alive. Because He lives, those who believe in Him will also be resurrected. Lord we are grateful. Blessings

248

Good Morning!

But the Lord is faithful, who will establish you and guard you from the evil one.
2 Thessalonians 3:3 NKJV

Because God is faithful, He could be trusted to strengthen the Thessalonians and protect them from Satan. Because God is faithful, He will not allow evil men to gain a victory over believers. Because God is faithful, He is still strengthening us daily and protecting us from the devices of Satan. We are forever grateful for His divine protection in our lives. Amen. Blessings

249

Good Morning!

Who is this King of glory? The Lord of hosts, He is the King of glory. **Psalm 24:10 NKJV**

The name "LORD of hosts" identifies the Lord as eternal and ruler over all the angels and stars. The title reflects the truth that, although Israel's earthly king was David, her real king was Yahweh. Prophetically, the glorious king who will enter Jerusalem is the Lord Jesus. He is the Lord of heaven. All glory to God for our Redeemer. Blessings

250

Good Morning!

Have you not known? Have you not heard? The everlasting God, the Lord, The Creator of the ends of the earth, Neither faints nor is weary.
His understanding is unsearchable.
Isaiah 40:28 NKJV

Israel continually sinned and rebelled against their covenant-keeping God through unbelief, and in their foolishness thought that God did not see their wickedness The rebellious and complaining nation needed to be reminded of who God is and that their God was the all-powerful Creator, the generous Provider, their strong Tower, their Shepherd, their Peace, and their Defender, their ever-present help in time of trouble. When the stresses and strains of life cause our faith to be tested, we need to remember who our everlasting, omniscient, gracious Creator God is, and of what He is truly capable. He understands. Blessings

251

Good Morning!

For with the heart one believes unto righteousness, and with the mouth confession is made unto salvation.
Romans 10:10 NKJV

Confession of Jesus as Lord is one of the earliest Christian confessions of faith. To acknowledge Jesus as Lord certainly involves a recognition of His deity, a recognition of His ability to save, and an acknowledgment of His sovereign right as God-Savior to demand obedience to Himself in all things. The idea of personally trusting Him is involved. Glory to God for our remedy of salvation. We are grateful. Blessings

252 Good Morning!

The generous soul will be made rich, And he who waters will also be watered himself. **Proverbs 11:25 NKJV**

Solomon extols the virtue of generosity. It pleases God when we lovingly serve others, including with material resources and care. Spiritually, we are guaranteed to see some benefit from doing good for others. In life, it's usually the case that generous people get help and support from others during hard times, unlike the greedy who are often ignored. The expected result of generous, loving kindness to others is reciprocal love and care. Let's strive to be generous, loving, and kind to those who find themselves in need. Thank you Lord. Blessings

253

Good Morning!

Cast your burden on the Lord, And He shall sustain you; He shall never permit the righteous to be moved.
Psalm 55:22 NKJV

As God lays burdens or other issues of life that God lays on us, we need to give it all back to Him. In His wisdom He places things on us, He wants us to use our wisdom to place it back in His capable hands. He gives us all a portion of suffering, we need to learn how to accept it with cheerful resignation, and then take it back to Him with assurance and confidence that He will make things well. Lord we glorify You even when we are called to suffer in this life. We are grateful. Amen. Blessings

254

Good Morning!

But without faith it is impossible to please Him, for he who comes to God must believe that He is, and that He is a rewarder of those who diligently seek Him. **Hebrew 11:6 NKJV**

Faith is certain of God's promise, it's confident of His power, it perceives the divine design for our lives, it acts on God's promises, it esteems Christ above all else, and it allows us to overcome tremendous odds. Lord thank You for Your faithfulness to us, Your goodness, Your grace and mercy. Because of Your divine wisdom, we honor You because You make it easy for us to have faith in You. We are grateful. Blessings

255

Good Morning!

For I know that my Redeemer lives, And He shall stand at last on the earth. **Job 19:25 NKJV**

In the midst of his pain, Job remained certain of the Lord he served and the relationship he shared with Him. Job's knowledge of the Lord should serve as a reminder to every believer, bringing hope even in the midst of our greatest trials. Job knew the Redeemer. He knew the Lord. He had a personal relationship with God. He had lost much that pertained to this physical life, but he had not lost his relationship with God. There is a profound realization that we see in Job's situation, not only did Job know the Redeemer, the Redeemer knew him. What are we learning from our tests and trials that are allowed by our Redeemer? Blessings

256

Good Morning!

You are the light of the world.
A city that is set on a hill cannot be hidden.
Matthew 5:14 NKJV

Spiritually speaking, there is no light in the world apart from Jesus Christ. His light, shines through every person who belongs to Him. In this way, the light of Christ is distributed into the darkness in every corner of humanity. Thank you Lord for allowing Your light to shine brightly within us. We are forever grateful. Blessings

257

Good Morning!

Let your speech always be with grace, seasoned with salt, that you may know how you ought to answer each one.
Colossians 4:6 NKJV

The believer's words are to preserve the message of Christ, helping it effectively reach as many people as possible. What a Christian says ought to add value to conversations, our words should be uplifting or helpful. Finally, the truth of our renewed Christian lives ought to be clear in the different flavor of how we speak and act. In order to give an answer in a truly Christian way, a person must present truth using proper words and a proper attitude. Thank you Lord for blessing my words with Your wisdom. Amen. Blessings

258 Good Morning!

These things I have spoken to you, that in Me you may have peace. In the world you will have tribulation; but be of good cheer, I have overcome the world. **John 16:33 NKJV**

This message is about the inner peace and the victory Christ gives His followers who rely on Him when we are faced with tribulation. Becoming a Christian does not guarantee an easy life. In fact, Jesus has made it clear that following Him can lead to persecution. The joy held by believers comes from knowing that Christ has already obtained ultimate victory, and nothing in this world can undo that. Lord we worship and praise You for the peace that we find only in You. Amen. Blessings

259

Good Morning!

Beloved, let us love one another, for love is of God; and everyone who loves is born of God and knows God.
1 John 4:7 NKJV

John is showing us that love is grounded in God's nature. Those who have been born of God ought to emulate His character. God provides both the source and example of the believer's love. Love for others is an integral part of our relationship with God. While no one has seen God, His love is evident in the work of Christ and in our love for others. Those who demonstrate godly love prove that they are saved. What are you demonstrating? Blessings

260

Good Morning!

Let us therefore come boldly unto the throne of grace, that we may obtain mercy, and find grace to help in time of need. **Hebrews 4:16 NKJV**

Knowing that Christ fully and personally understands what it means to be human gives us confidence when we bring Him our failures and needs. Jesus is seated at the right hand of the Father in heaven and we are invited to come before Him with boldness, so let us draw near with confidence to the throne of grace. We are encouraged to come to Him and to keep on coming to His throne, without fear or doubt. We are to come to Him freely, constantly, ceaselessly, and persistently. Whatever your need or desire is, boldly take it all to the altar, God hears you and He's willing and able to do exceedingly and abundantly more than we can think or ask. Be encouraged. Blessings

261

Good Morning!

But when the kindness and the love of God our Savior toward man appeared, ⁵ not by works of righteousness which we have done, but according to His mercy He saved us, through the washing of regeneration and renewing of the Holy Spirit. **Titus 3:4-5 NKJV**

God saved us through the water of rebirth and renewal by the Holy Spirit. Being saved is not something we accomplish through our good deeds, but through the mercy of God. The Holy Spirit renews our lives when we come to faith in Christ. Thank You Lord for your Spirit that continues to bless, sustain, and empower us as we strive to do Your will. Amen. Blessings

262

Good Morning!

My little children, let us not love in word or in tongue, but in deed and in truth. **1 John 3:18 NKJV**

John is talking about what we are to do when we see others in need. He told us to have active compassion: Let us not love in word or in our speech, but in deed. When we see a need, it's good to talk about it, but we must also do something about it. Let's strive to be the example our Lord has left and continue to love freely and in action. Blessings

263

Good Morning!

Now the Lord is the Spirit; and where the Spirit of the Lord is, there is liberty.
2 Corinthians 3:17 NKJV

With the power of the Holy Spirit living in us, we are being transformed into God's image. All who come to God through faith in Christ are forgiven for their sins and able to look on God's glory. Lord thank You for your Holy Spirit and the freedom that comes with having Your Spirit operating on the inside of us. Blessings

264

Good Morning!

Lead me in Your truth and teach me,
For You are the God of my salvation;
On You I wait all the day.
Psalm 25:5 NKJV

Our God is teaching us how to wait all day long for His goodness. We need to rely on Him to guide and teach us, we need to look to Him continually for direction, and we need to trust Him with a trust that isn't shaken by any worldly circumstances or concerns. Thank you Lord for being our salvation. Amen. Blessings

265

Good Morning!

He who keeps instruction is in the way of life, But he who refuses correction goes astray.
Proverbs 10:17 NKJV

Christ is the only true way to life, who, by His obedience, sufferings, and death, has opened the new and living way. All who reject the counsel and advice, the admonitions and reproofs, given in the word of God, will wander far from the way that leads to life, and go into the paths of sin that unfortunately, is the way of death. We must operate in obedience by following the instructions. Thank you Lord for mercy, guidance and direction.
Blessings

266

Good Morning!

He heals the brokenhearted
And binds up their wounds.
Psalm 147:3 NKJV

God is reminding us that He has not forgotten or neglected us. He will heal our broken hearts and make us strong again. Just like physical wounds can heal, internal ones, with time, can heal as well. Our Lord will restore our strength and make us better and stronger than we were before. We just need to trust in Him and speak to Him when the pain seems to become too much to handle. Our God is faithful and He is able. Blessings

267

Good Morning!

Let the peace of Christ rule in your hearts, since as members of one body you were called to peace. And be thankful.
Colossians 3:15 NKJV

God has done so much for us that we should seek to become increasingly grateful people. We receive peace with God through the blood of the cross. It is to rule in our hearts, meaning it should be in charge of how we live. Believers are not called to live in violence or squabbles among each other, but in peace. Lord teach us how to be thankful and grateful for the peace that You freely give to us. Amen. Blessings

268

Good Morning!

Therefore I will look to the Lord;
I will wait for the God of my salvation;
My God will hear me.
Micah 7:7 NKJV

Regardless of what we may be called to do, we must keep our focus on Him not the circumstances or issue. Wait for Him, He's the God of our salvation, He's always listening for our call and He's ready with an answer. Keep trusting, keep hoping, keep looking to Him, He's worthy. Blessings

269

Good Morning!

Now to Him who is able to do exceedingly abundantly above all that we ask or think, according to the power that works in us, 21 to Him be glory in the church by Christ Jesus to all generations, forever and ever. Amen. **Ephesians 3:20-21 NKJV**

No matter how bold our requests may seem, God can do all we ask and so much more. God's means for accomplishing more than we can imagine comes through His strength. His work is done by the Holy Spirit's power within us, rather than by our human strength. As Jesus taught His apostles, the spirit is always willing, but the flesh is weak. Let's strive to move past our flesh and operate more in the spirit that lives within us so that we can accomplish greater works and bring more glory to our God. Blessings

270

Good Morning!

But I say to you who hear: Love your enemies, do good to those who hate you, 28 bless those who curse you, and pray for those who spitefully use you.
Luke 6:27-28 NKJV

It doesn't make sense to work towards the best for someone who actively wants to cause hardship and disappointment in our lives. This is only possible, in an emotionally healthy way, if our focus is not on our enemy but on our God and His promises. Lord keep us in a posture to always love our enemies, offer blessings to those who curse our very existence, and pray for those who willfully and spitefully use us. Others will look at us and try to figure out how we can allow someone to use us to that extent, how can we let them get away with treating us that way, don't be dismayed because it's the God in us that is being used and abused. Woe to them, when it's time to answer to Him. Teach us Lord, to consistently show these people the mighty God who lives, breathes, and moves on the inside of us. Blessings

271

Good Morning!

with all lowliness and gentleness, with longsuffering, bearing with one another in love
Ephesians 4:2 NKJV

God has called us to walk in unity and to walk worthy of the honor of being called by the Master. He has called us to be humble, gentle, and patient as we represent Him in this life. With the help of the Holy Spirit, is how we should handle the faults and failures of those around us. God has equipped us with these fruits of the spirit to help us stand firm in His Will and the way that He will have us to go. Let's strive to respond and react with humility, gentleness, and patience more than we do at this time. Lord we are grateful for the example that you have set for us. Blessings

272

Good Morning!

But I will sing of Your power; Yes, I will sing aloud of Your mercy in the morning; For You have been my defense And refuge in the day of my trouble. **Psalm 59:16 NKJV**

God is perfect and loves us despite our imperfections or the struggles we face. His love is a mighty fortress and refuge for us all. When we rely on God as our defense in all things, He will put a song of joy in our heart. We are so thankful and so grateful for the strength and joy of the Lord that lives in us and allows us to overcome the different obstacles of life. Blessings

273

Good Morning!

There are many devices in a man's heart; nevertheless the counsel of the Lord, that shall stand.
Proverbs 19:21 NKJV

This scripture reminds us to submit to the plans of God. So God we yield our plans to you today, we lay our plans down and we pray that you have your way in our lives. Have your way in our attitude, have your way in our families, have your way in our churches, have your way with us as we pray and seek your guidance. We are grateful. Blessings

274

Good Morning!

But let justice run down like water,
And righteousness like a mighty stream.
Amos 5:24 NKJV

God wanted His chosen people to obey Him, by ruling justly and behaving righteously, to stop living as hypocrites and idolaters and return to Him. This point is clarified by John in 1 John 4:8, "anyone who does not love does not know God, because God is love." God is calling on His people to have the love for Him and for others that we once did. Let's get back to the basics as we operate in the love of God in all situations and circumstances. Blessings

275

Good Morning!

Let nothing be done through strife or vainglory; but in lowliness of mind let each esteem other better than themselves.
Philippians 2:3 NKJV

We are called to do nothing from selfish ambition, we should act in humility in all things and count others more significant than ourselves. We need to strive to be humble before others and not think of ourselves in the process. God when it comes to our ambition and our motivation for the things we do today, help us to do it in a selfless way, not thinking about ourselves but thinking about the significance of others and ultimately thinking about the significance of Your glory and the powerful example You set on the cross. We are grateful. Blessings

276

Good Morning!

But if the Spirit of Him who raised Jesus from the dead dwells in you, He who raised Christ from the dead will also give life to your mortal bodies through His Spirit who dwells in you.
Romans 8:11 NKJV

As Christians, we are not in the flesh but in the Spirit, because the Spirit of God dwells within us, we have a new identity and new opportunities to obey God. We now live with the Spirit of God, and He is an ever-present Helper. Anyone who does not have the Spirit of Christ living in them, does not belong to God. He sent the Spirit as a Helper. So, we have the Holy Spirit with and in us, acting as a leader, but we must be willing to follow. Are you willing to follow? Blessings

277

Good Morning!

Behold, how good and how pleasant it is
For brethren to dwell together in unity!
Psalm 133:1 NKJV

This was a hymn of praise that would echo throughout the land of Israel, as God's people traveled towards their sacred destination. We are all on our march towards our heavenly home, so every step we make should be one that allows us to live together with our brothers and sisters in Christ in gracious harmony and godly unity. In the Body of Christ there should be a oneness of spirit on the essential fundamentals of our faith, where minor issues don't cause discord and division. Small disagreements or alternative views on minor issues should be approached with wisdom and grace. Thank you Lord for blessing us with a patient, kind and gracious spirit of love that comes from the indwelling of the Holy Spirit. We are grateful. Blessings

278

Good Morning!

Finally, brethren, whatever things are true, whatever things are noble, whatever things are just, whatever things are pure, whatever things are lovely, whatever things are of good report, if there is any virtue and if there is anything praiseworthy meditate on these things. **Philippians 4:8 NKJV**

In this scripture, Paul is encouraging us to focus on the good and honorable things in the world as opposed to the lies that Satan tries to weave into our lives daily. Children of God should continuously think about the things above, while God guards our hearts because keeping our focus on the positive attributes of God, pleases Him to the utmost. Thank you Lord for teaching us to trust You as well as serve and honor You in a positive way each day. We are grateful. Blessings

279

Good Morning!

But do not forget to do good and to share, for with such sacrifices God is well pleased.
Hebrews 12:16 NKJV

We are commanded to do good to others. This should never be presented as a means to obtain salvation, or to earn redemption from our God. On the contrary, Scripture makes it very clear that good deeds cannot rescue us from sin. The sacrifice of Jesus is the thing that can justify us before God. When we accept Him, by faith, we can be reconciled with God. Good works, are the natural, expected outcome of our relationship with Him. Lord we thank you. Blessings

280

Good Morning!

Is anyone among you suffering? Let him pray. Is anyone cheerful? Let him sing psalms.
James 5:13 NKJV

When we are going through our season of suffering, we need to find the strength of the Holy Spirit to pray for ourselves and praise God in the midst of our suffering. When all things concerning us appear to be going well, when we understand that the joy of the Lord is our strength, and we can go out and be proud to witness to others, we need to worship and praise God even the more. During our times of spiritual weakness when depression tries to abound in our lives, let's seek the face of God, touch and agree with those who are genuine and sincere in their walk with Christ and pray until our change comes. Prayer and praise is still working in our favor. All glory be to God. Be encouraged. Blessings

281

Good Morning!

And the light shines in the darkness, and the darkness did not comprehend it.
John 1:5 NKJV

Because of sin, darkness entered the heart of man, but it is through the Light of God's Son, that sin, death, and darkness has been overcome. When Jesus came into the world as the Light of Life, He came to shine His light of love on every man who chose to accept Him, but many of the people who were closest to Him couldn't comprehend His brightness. They had a hard time separating the Jesus they knew before from the beacon of Light and goodness whom He had transformed into to. Lord we thank for delivering us from the darkness, thank You for the sacrifice of Your Son, thank You for renewing the right spirit in us, and thank you for placing us in a posture to understand and believe with Jesus on the inside darkness can't find a resting place. We glorify You. Blessings

282

Good Morning!

As a father pities his children,
So the Lord pities those who fear Him.
Psalm 103:13 NKJV

We serve a good and kind Heavenly Father, who demonstrates genuine compassion for us. God understands what we face, and He cares for us. The sleeping child needs to be sheltered, weary children need to be carried. Hungry children need their father's provision of food to sustain them, while the wandering child needs to be looked after, taken home, and shown much understanding. The disobedient child needs to be chastened, and the child that is wounded and afraid needs the loving compassion that can only come from the heart of a loving and compassionate Father. Thank you Lord for showing us what care and compassion looks like. Blessings

283

Good Morning!

For we are His workmanship, created in Christ Jesus for good works, which God prepared beforehand that we should walk in them. **Ephesians 2:10 NKJV**

When we live our lives according to God's purpose, we bring glory to our Master and Creator. This statement offers us excellent insight into what God desires from us after salvation. God crafted us with skill and intricate detail, for His purpose. We are created for His good work, we must remember, good works can't save us but they are meant to be the result of our salvation. Lord bless us to live up to your expectations and to be mindful of our good works our desire is to please you daily. Blessings

284

Good Morning!

Be diligent to present yourself approved to God, a worker who does not need to be ashamed, rightly dividing the word of truth.
2 Timothy 2:15 NKJV

As we commit more to the work of the Lord, our challenge is not only to be approved, but to be a worker "who has no need to be ashamed of the gospel." As we are called to go through our times of suffering, and persecution, we should focus on being bold in our faith and try not to avoid hardship and persecution. As children of God, we must study the word seeking God's face and understanding as we do so that we can boldly and rightly handle the word of truth and be strengthened by the word, as we go through. We are grateful for the word. Blessings

285

Good Morning!

Come to Me, all you who labor and are heavy laden, and I will give you rest.
Matthew 11:28 NKJV

This is an invitation to salvation for all of us who are tired, weary, and weighted down with the problems of life. This is a reminder that in spite of life happening, we can have a solid relationship with our Lord and Savior. We are reminded that following Christ means taking on difficult circumstances and giving up our worldly desires. From the view of eternal salvation, following Christ means understanding the impossible task of carrying the weight of our sin. Thank you Lord for being our heavy load bearer and for giving us rest in every situation. We are grateful. Blessings

286 Good Morning!

Blessed be the God and Father of our Lord Jesus Christ, the Father of mercies and God of all comfort, 4 who comforts us in all our tribulation, that we may be able to comfort those who are in any trouble, with the comfort with which we ourselves are comforted by God.
2 Corinthians 1:3-4 NKJV

This scripture reminds us that we serve a God who comforts us in our time of need. He is the father of mercies and the God of comfort. He is the God and Ruler of all comfort. He is the father of mercies and He consistently comforts us in the midst our afflictions. So, when He brings others across our path, He expects us to to comfort and encourage them. Let's strive to build one another up rather than tear down. Thank you Lord for a heart of compassion. Blessings

287

Good Morning!

He restores my soul; He leads me in the paths of righteousness For His name's sake.
Psalm 26:3 NKJV

In this scripture, David credits the Lord, his shepherd, with restoring or refreshing his soul. In Bible times, if a sheep became injured, its shepherd would treat its wounds until its good health returned. It's a blessing to have our Savior who restores us to good spiritual health after the evil world hurts us, or when we have hurt ourselves by failing to follow Him closely. Thank you Lord for guiding us along the right path so that we may bring glory and honor to your name. We are grateful. Blessings

288

Good Morning!

He who walks with wise men will be wise, But the companion of fools will be destroyed. **Proverbs 13:20**

This scripture reminds us that it is extremely important to choose our friends and associates wisely. We must be careful about who we allow in our circle, those we hang out with. If those whom we walk with are wise and consistently strive to make good righteous choices, then we will be drawn to live righteously as well. Are you striving to be an example of righteous living for those who are following you? Blessings

289

Good Morning!

For to be carnally minded is death, but to be spiritually minded is life and peace. **Romans 8:6 NKJV**

In this scripture, Paul is describing the difference between living by the flesh, where we strive to satisfy our selfish, sinful human wants and desires and what it means to be spiritually minded, this mind helps us to be spiritually oriented, so that we will learn to live by the Spirit of the Most High God. If we set our mind on the spirit and walk according to the spirit, we'll not only experience life and peace but we'll be positioned to live the divine life that Christ desires for us. Thank you Lord for a submissive mind, an humble heart, and a loving desire to always do what's good in Your sight. We are forever grateful. Blessings

290

Good Morning!

Blessed be the Lord,
Who daily loads us with benefits,
The God of our salvation! Selah
Psalm 68:19 NKJV

We all carry heavy burdens daily, but God promises to carry us. He desires to lift us up, carry and comfort us, and ultimately save us. He will do all of this daily, if we let Him. Christ carried our sin to the grave, so we are assured that He will carry us through today. Because God raised Jesus from the dead, we are assured that He will raise our heads above today's high waters. Our issues and pain can sometimes make today feel unbearable, but God has made us a promise, when we meet the unbearable, He will bear us up daily. Lord, thank you for reminding us that your compassions never fail, your steadfast love never ceases, and your mercies are new every morning. We are grateful. Blessings

291

Good Morning!

For it is God who works in you both to will and to do for His good pleasure.
Philippians 2:13 NKJV

God moves through the lives of believers. Completely comprehending this concept, should lead believers to a deep sense of awe and appreciation for our Lord and Savior. Having God's Spirit within us, gives us both the desire and the strength to live a life that is pleasing to Him. Obtaining His good pleasure requires faith, belief, and obedience. Thank you Lord for a posture of obedience to your will. Thank you for placing us in posture of obedience that is based on our love for You which is in turn based on the Spirit that lives within us. We are thankful. Blessings

292

Good Morning!

Beloved, if God so loved us,
we also ought to love one another.
1 John 4-11 NKJV

This kind of love is possible only if we have the life of God within us. With His love operating on the inside, we can love like this, unconditionally and we should. That is the point of it all. Thank you Lord for reminding us that we must love one another in all situations and circumstances. We are grateful. Blessings

293

Good Morning!

Blessed is the man who endures temptation; for when he has been approved, he will receive the crown of life which the Lord has promised to those who love Him. **James 1:12 NKJV**

When we are called for our season of tribulation and suffering, as believers, we go through with our Lord and Savior close by. We give all glory to God for His grace, mercy, and faithfulness because in the midst of our tests and trials, He continues to cover us, protect us, and keep us safe. Believers who suffer through the trials of life are sure to receive a future blessing from God. These blessings will far exceed any blessing we can gain from the world and we have an opportunity to be strengthened as we go through. Thank you Lord for the process of our suffering and tribulations. Blessings

294

Good Morning!

Therefore be imitators of God as dear children.
Ephesians 5:1 NKJV

He didn't just call us as His children, He loves us because we are His children and He has created us to have a close relationship with Him, a relationship that should lead us to imitate Him in all aspects of our lives. Thank you Lord for reminding us that we are called to be like You to follow Your example, to imitate Your life and character, to grow in grace, and to be conformed into Your likeness each day. We are forever grateful. Blessings

295

Good Morning!

And we know that all things work together for good to those who love God, to those who are the called according to His purpose.
Romans 8:28 NKJV

Our God is always thinking about the end result, the big picture. In this scripture, He is reminding us and reassuring us that all things are working out for our good. Sometimes, we have different situations or circumstances to happen in our lives that at times, seem unfair or unfortunate. When we are in the midst, we often focus on the issue instead of the lessons we may learn from going through the process. We want to encourage you as we encourage ourselves, on today to look to God for guidance as we go through the test and trials of life, focus more on Him and less on the issues, and ask Him to reveal the lessons we should learn as live, move, and breathe daily. We are thankful. Blessings

296

Good Morning!

Oh, give thanks to the Lord!
Call upon His name; Make known
His deeds among the peoples!
Psalm 105:1 NKJV

We need to always be thankful and show thanks to the Lord. We can call on Him at any time and in every situation, He will answer because He has already prepared a way of escape or He has already equipped us to stand strong in the midst of our situation. After He has come to deliver us, we need to share our story with all who will listen, because our testimony may have the foundation of strength and power to help propel someone else to trust God when they are ready to give up. Let's strive to let the world know how good our Savior truly is. Amen. Blessings

297

Good Morning!

Therefore humble yourselves under the mighty hand of God, that He may exalt you in due time
1 Peter 5:6 NKJV

Humility is a fruit of the Spirit that should be the goal of all Christians. It doesn't matter how mature we may be in our faith or how young we are in our Christian walk, if we are humble, God will extend grace to us as well as wisdom, faith, understanding, and greater holiness. A spirit of humility is pleasing to our Lord because it is the spirit that represents our Savior. Christ was a man that humbled Himself, in the power of the Holy Spirit, under the mighty hand of the Father, and at the proper time He was lifted up. As we follow the example of Christ, we must meekly take up our cross, in the power of the Spirit, and humble ourselves under the mighty hand of God so that we may have the opportunity to grow in the grace and knowledge of our Savior and at the proper time, God will raise us up. We are thankful for a spirit of humility. Blessings

298

Good Morning!

that He would grant you, according to the riches of His glory, to be strengthened with might through His Spirit in the inner man,
Ephesians 3:16 NKJV

God desires for us to be strong enough to resist temptation. In an effort to help us resist temptation, He will use the Spirit of God to infuse strength into our inner man through His Spirit. We are inspired and forever grateful that God is always available to strengthen us by the power of the Holy Spirit. Blessings

299

Good Morning!

that if you confess with your mouth the Lord Jesus and believe in your heart that God has raised Him from the dead, you will be saved. **Romans 10:9 NKJV**

Confessing that Jesus is Lord is more than just speaking some words, it's a public declaration of our allegiance to Christ This confession is an essential part of our faith because it demonstrates our willingness to identify with Jesus and humbly submit to His lordship in our lives. Anyone who trusts in Christ for his or her salvation will surely agree that Christ is Lord and He was raised from the dead. This person will most definitely be saved. Lord, thank you for a path to salvation that has been blazed by our Savior. Blessings

300

Good Morning!

This is My commandment, that you love one another as I have loved you.
John 15:12 NKJV

In this scripture, Jesus is not telling believers to feel about others the way He does. Neither is He demanding we be sinless and perfect in our actions. He is telling us that our love needs to echo the character of His love. We need to understand that the love Jesus speaks of is practical, not emotional. We don't have to "feel warm thoughts" for others, but we do need to act lovingly towards them, even when they are hostile towards us. Sometimes affection will grow as we serve others. But, even when it doesn't, the command to love is still the ultimate goal. Lord thank you for a heart to love others just like You love us. We are grateful. Blessings

301

Good Morning!

The Lord is near to those who have a broken heart, And saves such as have a contrite spirit.
Psalm 34:18 NKJV

This psalm is reminding us that God is not only present with us, but He's always near. He's near and He understands the pain we feel. He's also near to comfort us during our time of loss when we find it difficult to put into words the ache we feel as we go through. Thank you Lord for being close to those who are brokenhearted and we are forever grateful to you for saving those of us who are crushed in our spirit. All glory to God for His goodness. Blessings

302

Good Morning!

But none of these things move me; nor do I count my life dear to myself, so that I may finish my race with joy, and the ministry which I received from the Lord Jesus, to testify to the gospel of the grace of God. **Acts 20:24 NKJV**

We are on this earth to spread the gospel of the grace of God. We are also here to help other people know and understand how good, great, gracious, and glorious our God truly is. Thank you Lord for the opportunity to be a beacon of light in this world. Thank you for placing your word in our heart. Thank you for the opportunity to run this Christian race with joy and diligence to the testament of the gospel. Amen. Blessings

303

Good Morning!

The Lord your God in your midst, The Mighty One, will save; He will rejoice over you with gladness, He will quiet you with His love, He will rejoice over you with singing." **Zephaniah 3:17 NKJV**

Our God is more than the Creator, He is Lord of all, He is God, He is in the midst of us; loving us, caring for us, protecting us, defending us, indwelling us with His presence. He died so that we might have life and have it more abundantly. God's Word to us is sure, steadfast, faithful, and true. He is always near to help, to heal, to hold, and to carry us in His everlasting arms. We are so thankful and so grateful to serve a God like Him. Blessings

304

Good Morning!

Enter into His gates with thanksgiving,
And into His courts with praise.
Be thankful to Him, and bless
His name. **Psalm 100:4 NKJV**

When we come to God, we have numerous reasons to thank Him. Our Lord and Savior, Jesus is the greatest of all these reasons. Bringing thankfulness and praise to God is a way for us to worship and praise Him to the utmost. Let's enter His gates with thanksgiving and His courts with praise on this day. Because tomorrow is not promised to any of us. Blessings

305

Good Morning!

Be diligent to present yourself approved to God, a worker who does not need to be ashamed, rightly dividing the word of truth. **2 Timothy 2:15 NKJV**

As we commit more to the work of the Lord, our challenge is not only to be approved, but to be a worker "who has no need to be ashamed of the gospel." As we are called to go through our times of suffering, and persecution, we should focus on being bold in our faith and try not to avoid hardship and persecution. As children of God, we must study the word seeking God's face and understanding as we do so that we can boldly and rightly handle the word of truth and be strengthened by the word, as we go through. We are grateful for the word. Blessings

306

Good Morning!

But if we walk in the light as He is in the light, we have fellowship with one another, and the blood of Jesus Christ His Son cleanses us from all sin.
1 John 1:7 NKJV

As Christians, we abide in the light of Christ because He is the light of the world. When we walk according to His will, we are positioned to lovingly fellowship with one another. In the dark areas of our lives, we ask our Savior to shine the light of His love. Darkness has to flee when the light of the Holy Spirit shows up. Because the light shines brightly on the inside of us illuminating our path, we have access to the power of the Blood of Jesus. The Blood that cleanses us of our sin. The Blood that soothes our troubled souls. Glory. Thank you Lord for the light that makes our enemies back up and the Blood that washes away the residue of blackness from our souls. Blessings

307

Good Morning!

Now may the God of patience and comfort grant you to be like-minded toward one another, according to Christ Jesus.
Romans 15:5 NKJV

God is a source of endurance and encouragement for us. He will help us to keep moving forward when we want to give up. He will sustain us as we follow the path He has predestined for us. God is patient and forgiving. When we are weak, He lifts us with encouragement and with endurance to keep moving forward. He wants us to strive to be more like Him daily. We want to encourage you on this day to keep pressing toward the mark of the high call of God in Christ Jesus. He has a greater reward for you. Be encouraged. Blessings

308

Good Morning!

No one is holy like the Lord,
For there is none besides You,
Nor is there any rock like our God.
1 Samuel 2:2 NKJV

There is no other being in the universe that is Holy like our God. No other God even exists that can measure up like our God. He is God all by Himself. He is the only Ruler in all the earth who deserves our praise and our worship. Let's strive to always exalt God in all that we do. Only He is worthy, no one cares and loves us the way He does. We are so thankful and so grateful for the opportunity to lift Him up before everything else. Blessings

309

Good Morning!

while we do not look at the things which are seen, but at the things which are not seen. For the things which are seen are temporary, but the things which are not seen are eternal.
2 Corinthians 4:18 NKJV

Every now and then, affliction (bodily pain or mental distress), will show up unexpected, uninvited, and definitely unwanted in our lives. When it's our turn to go thru and because we are caught off guard, we feel like we might not make it out of this one. We come to encourage you today, that which you are going through, has been allowed by God, He knew it was coming and please believe, He prepared you for it. The pain, the stress, the mental anguish, is temporary. God wants you to humble yourself before Him on this day, pray like you have never prayed before, seek His face in the midst of your affliction, and turn from all that is not like Him and pleasing in His sight, and you will hear His voice clearly (2 Chronicles 7:14). You will hear Him encouraging you and letting you know that everything is already alright. God needed your undivided attention, He has it today, He wants to heal you from the inside out, He wants to fill you up with His goodness. In order to get to His eternal goodness, He is allowing affliction to touch your life, but it's temporary. Our God is a healer and He's already started to heal you and everyone around you. Some healing has to take place on the other side. Don't fear the eternal healing because it comes with peace, freedom, and the strength of our Lord and Savior. Be encouraged. Blessings

310

Good Morning!

"You are worthy, O Lord,
To receive glory and honor and power;
For You created all things, And by Your will they exist and were created."
Revelation 4:14 NKJV

This verse assures us that creation came into existence because it was God's will. Clearly, creation doesn't exist by accident. God spoke everything into existence through His will. Every human being owes his or her existence to God's creative work. The phrase Mother Nature is popular, but it is an incorrect reference to the natural world. The living and true God is the Creator, and He is worthy to receive all of our praise. We are grateful to be able to extend everlasting praises to Him. Blessings

311

Good Morning!

So then neither he who plants is anything, nor he who waters, but God who gives the increase. 8 Now he who plants and he who waters are one, and each one will receive his own reward according to his own labor.
1 Corinthians 3:7-8 NKJV

Paul used the gardening metaphor to explain how the gospel is spread. He let us know that he planted the seed of the gospel, Apollos came behind him and watered it. But God, is the one who caused it to grow. We will encounter different emphasis and different styles as to how others deliver the gospel, please understand this does not mean that one individual is more godly or more important than the other. Christian leaders who are called to build the church will have their work judged by Christ to see if they have built on the solid foundation of Christ. On that great getting up morning, all human wisdom will be shown to be futile and worthless. We are so grateful and so thankful to God for the increase. Amen. Blessings

312

Good Morning!

For I, the Lord your God, will hold your right hand, Saying to you, 'Fear not, I will help you.'
Isaiah 41:13 NKJV

God takes hold of our 'right hand'. Why the right hand? The majority of us are right-handed. Our right hand is the hand of strength, of authority, of sovereignty, of blessings and most importantly, of friendship. God takes our right hand because His relationship with us is just that close. Our divine parent and God is telling us, 'Do not fear, I will help you. These simple words, of great comfort, are for those of us who believe, so the terror of the darkness is taken away when He holds our right hand as we go through daily. Lord, we are so grateful to have you close to us. Blessings grateful to be able to extend everlasting praises to Him. Blessings

313

Good Morning!

We love Him because He first loved us.
1 John 4:19 NKJV

God loved us, before we were capable of loving Him, and we can only love others because of what He has done in our lives. John is warning us if we can't agape love (love that is given whether or not it's returned) people who we can see, we are certainly unable to love God, who we are unable to see. Thank you Lord for a loving and kind heart. Blessings

314

Good Morning!

And do not be conformed to this world, but be transformed by the renewing of your mind, that you may prove what is that good and acceptable and perfect will of God. **Romans 12:2 NKJV**

This scripture is reminding us that we live out God's will when we change our thoughts to His thoughts, rather than living like the world dictates. The world will always pressure us into living sinful, selfish lives, but to live the good life that God desires for us, requires us to change how we behave, by changing how we think. Lord we honor and glorify You for changing our hearts and our thought patterns to align more to Your will. Hallelujah. Blessings

315

Good Morning!

Most assuredly, I say to you,
he who hears My word and believes in Him
who sent Me has everlasting life,
and shall not come into judgment,
but has passed from death into life.
John 5:24 NKJV

This scripture means Christians don't have to wait for eternal life to begin when we die or when our Savior returns, just like God promises in this passage. For the Christian, eternal life begins when we believe in "Him who sent" Jesus. Those who believe will repent and put their faith in Christ and begin living at the moment we believe. Lord we praise You for the power of the word that continues to change our lives, cleanse us, and make us free as we believe in You. We are grateful. Blessings

316

Good Morning!

Be of good courage,
And He shall strengthen your heart,
All you who hope in the Lord.
Psalm 31:24 NKJV

Don't be shy and afraid when Satan carries out his deceitful schemes and make you face the dangers and tribulations of this world, because God is for you, and He is right by your side through it all. Please know that you can trust Him, and rely on Him, despite your failures. Even when you get frustrated and angry with Him, when He allows you to go through He forgives you, because He knows that you are weak. Thank you Lord for covering and keeping us daily. Blessings

317

Good Morning!

By humility and the fear of the Lord Are riches and honor and life.
Proverbs 22:4 NKJV

Humility leads to the fear of the Lord, those who behave humbly towards others learn to fear the Lord, and be truly spiritual. Also these attributes are considered graces of the Spirit of God, that go together, where there is one, there is the other. Whoever is humbled under a sense of sin, and his own unworthiness, often fear the Lord; and those who fear the Lord, and His goodness, will walk humbly before Him. All who walk humbly before the Lord, will receive the spirit of humility that flows from the grace of God. The consequences of humility are riches, and honour, and life. These positive qualities allow us to honor God and treat others right both now and during everlasting life in the world to come. Thank you Lord. Blessings

318

Good Morning!

Likewise the Spirit also helps in our weaknesses. For we do not know what we should pray for as we ought, but the Spirit Himself makes intercession for us with groanings which cannot be uttered.
Romans 8:26 NKJV

Among the benefits of adoption into God's family is the special supernatural care bestowed on us by the Holy Spirit. The Holy Spirit is present within all Christians to assist us in those moments of moral, physical, and emotional weakness. We often confront difficulties so insurmountable that we don't know how to approach a prayer skillfully. We know we need to go to God, but we have already said all that we know to say to Him. In these times, the promise is that the Holy Spirit will make intercession for us with groanings that cannot be uttered. This communication is nonverbal but clearly understood by our God. We are grateful for the Holy Spirit that communicates on our behalf when are not able speak. Blessings

319

Good Morning!

I sought the Lord, and He heard me, And delivered me from all my fears. 5 They looked to Him and were radiant, And their faces were not ashamed.
Psalm 34:4-5 NKJV

As we seek God, He answers us. He delivers us, and takes away all our fears. The psalmist was not alone when he fled to Abimelech, so the meaning here is that they all looked to God, and found light and comfort in Him. Lord we thank you for encouraging us to look to You for strength and comfort in our times of weakness. We are grateful. Blessings

320

Good Morning!

Blessed are those who mourn,
For they shall be comforted.
Matthew 5:4 NKJV

Those who mourn, by definition, are not happy. Jesus wants us to understand that those of us who experience mourning are not hopeless. Sadness in life is not the result of sin. It comes from living on a planet ruled by death. Of all the people who mourn, those in Christ are blessed because they will be comforted by God in the here and now and they will be free from mourning for eternity. Lord, we are forever grateful. Blessings

321

Good Morning!

Blessed are the meek,
For they shall inherit the earth.
Matthew 5:5 NKJV

Meekness is not a requirement for becoming a Christian, but it is something that comes naturally from having a relationship with Christ. True meekness takes courage so we have to fight with ourselves to trust God's plan and His way. It's hard to be humble and patient when you don't fully understand how much you will win in the end. Thank you Lord for giving us the strength to trust you to win our battles rather than going to extremes to try to win on our own terms. We are grateful. Blessings

322

Good Morning!

Blessed are those who mourn,
For they shall be comforted.
Matthew 5:4 NKJV

Those who mourn, by definition, are not happy. Jesus wants us to understand that those of us who experience mourning are not hopeless. Sadness in life is not the result of sin. It comes from living on a planet ruled by death. Of all the people who mourn, those in Christ are blessed because they will be comforted by God in the here and now and they will be free from mourning for eternity. Lord, we are forever grateful. Blessing

323

Good Morning!

Blessed are the meek,
For they shall inherit the earth.
Matthew 5:5 NKJV

Meekness is not a requirement for becoming a Christian, but it is something that comes naturally from having a relationship with Christ. True meekness takes courage so we have to fight with ourselves to trust God's plan and His way. It's hard to be humble and patient when you don't fully understand how much you will win in the end. Thank you Lord for giving us the strength to trust you to win our battles rather than going to extremes to try to win on our own terms. We are grateful. Blessings

324

Good Morning!

Blessed are the pure in heart,
For they shall see God.
Matthew 5:8 NKJV

Instead of focusing on and striving to be pure on the outside, Jesus is telling us to focus on having a pure heart. Those who do this will see God, meaning we will see God's intentions and desires for us, and we will better understand the love He has for us. The pure in heart are focused from the inside out on one single thing. In this case, that thing is God. Don't lose focus, we have a great reward waiting for us. All glory to God. Blessings

325

Good Morning!

Blessed are the peacemakers,
For they shall be called sons of God.
Matthew 5:9 NKJV

This verse specifically calls Christians to obedience in being a peacemaker with others inside and outside the church. This means we are held accountable to how we react in traffic, how we communicate with one another, and how we respond when something is done that we don't agree with. Thank you Lord for a heart that always strives to reconcile those around us who are in conflict. We are grateful. Blessings

326

Good Morning!

Blessed are those who are persecuted for righteousness' sake, For theirs is the kingdom of heaven.
Matthew 5:10 NKJV

Those who are persecuted for righteousness sake, should continue to make a conscious choice to honor God, and to be faithful to Him, in spite of being persecuted by individuals who choose to be unrighteous. Regardless of how hard the situations may be we are blessed so keep doing what is right and we will experience eternal good in the kingdom of heaven. All glory to God. Blessings

327

Good Morning!

For His anger is but for a moment, His favor is for life; Weeping may endure for a night, But joy comes in the morning.
Psalm 30:5 NKJV

The discipline of the Lord is never pleasant and His anger does not last forever but His favor is for life. Joy really does come in the morning. Lord bless us to always understand that our morning is on the way and teach us to trust You and the plan you have for our lives in confidence . We are grateful. Blessings

328

Good Morning!

The things which you learned and received and heard and saw in me, these do, and the God of peace will be with you.
Philippians 4:9 NKJV

We are all products of our environment. We have learned from our parents, grandparents, friends, and associates how to do things the right way and the wrong way. As ambassadors for Christ, we are being encouraged to take those things that we have learned and represent our Savior in a positive light. Jesus's example served as a living teaching tool to all believers. Let's strive to mimic his approach and put the things that we have learned, received, heard, and saw into action so that we can show others how to Christ representatives on a daily basis. Amen. Blessings

329

Good Morning!

Jesus said to him, "You shall love the Lord your God with all your heart, with all your soul, and with all your mind.' ³⁸This is the first and great commandment. ³⁹And the second is like it: 'You shall love your neighbor as yourself.'
Matthew 22:37-39 NKJV

These scriptures need no explanation. We need to meditate on them and ask our Lord and Savior to teach us how to live them daily. Be encouraged. Blessings

330

Good Morning!

So then, my beloved brethren, let every man be swift to hear, slow to speak, slow to wrath.
James 1:19 NKJV

Slow to wrath means carefully gathering all the facts before choosing whether or not we should be angry. If we don't manage anger properly, it will negatively impact our relationship with God and with others. Because exhibiting righteous anger is difficult, it's not impossible. Rather than letting our anger be a foothold for the enemy, we can use. God's Spirit to help us rightly judge, maintain a pure motive, and be angry without sinning. Let's strive to take the time to hear to get a better understanding, and to think before we speak, this may keep the peace. Amen. Blessings

331

Good Morning!

Let no one despise your youth, but be an example to the believers in word, in conduct, in love, in spirit, in faith, in purity.
1 Timothy 4:12 NKJV

This is Paul's advice to Timothy. He's encouraging him to not give others the opportunity to think that him being young was a reason to believe he was anything but trustworthy, godly, and responsible. Timothy needed to represent himself so well that the people wouldn't have time to think about his age but they would respect his maturity in the Lord and receive from him. Thank you Lord for another example on how we should respond when you use younger individuals to speak and teach your word. We honor you. Blessings

332

Good Morning!

Therefore be merciful, just as your Father also is merciful.
Luke 6:36 NKJV

Jesus is saying, what we send into the lives of others will eventually come back into our own. We have been set apart for the service of Christ so we are commanded to walk in the way that God desires us to walk. We must be mindful and very much aware, as we strive to follow the positive attributes that we have been instructed to imitate, one of the most important attributes is extending mercy. We serve a God who extends new mercies to us daily, but many would rather withhold this powerful attribute than extend it to a sister or brother in the time of their need. We pray that this mindset is not embedded in your spirit. Be encouraged. Blessings

333

Good Morning!

And he will turn the hearts of the fathers to the children, And the hearts of the children to their fathers, Lest I come and strike the earth with a curse.
Malachi 4:6 NKJV

In this passage of scripture, fathers are our dead ancestors who died without the privilege of receiving the gospel, but they received the promise that the time would come when that privilege would be given to them. Malachi explained that Elijah is coming before that great and terrible Day of the Lord, to call His people to repentance and restoration: "He will restore the hearts of the fathers to their children and the hearts of children to their fathers." If not, God declared, He would come and strike the land with the curse. Those of you who have not trusted Christ for your redemption, will have to face the great and dreadful Day of the Lord, when the full force of God's wrath will be poured out on this Christ-rejecting, sinful world. Thank you Lord for a mind and a heart to receive the call. Blessings

334

Good Morning!

Now all things are of God, who has reconciled us to Himself through Jesus Christ, and has given us the ministry of reconciliation. **2 Corinthians 5:18 NKJV**

Once Paul understood that Christ died to pay for human sin, Paul saw that those who are "in Christ" are entirely new creatures. This happens only when someone comes to Christ through faith and by God's grace (Ephesians 2:8-9). The old, sinful version of those is over. Through faith in Christ, any person can be reconciled to God. By using the word reconciled, Paul means our separation from God caused by sin can be removed, once and for all. Forgiven for all our sin, we become fully welcomed into a relationship with God. Lord we honor and praise You for relationship on this day. Blessings

335

Good Morning!

But seek first the kingdom of God and His righteousness, and all these things shall be added to you.
Matthew 6:33 NKJV

God has told us as plainly as He could that we should not worry or fret over what we will eat, drink, or wear because He knows that we need all of these things. So because He knows what we need, we don't have to ask for these things. His desire is to always meet everyone of our needs. But what He desires first from each of us regardless of whether or not our earthly needs are met, is that we will make Him a priority by seeking Him, His kingdom, and His righteousness before all else and He will take care of everything else. He will bless us to lie down in green pastures, He will make the crooked places straight in our lives, He will renew the right spirit within us, He will strengthen our resolve to do His will, He will bless us with spiritual prosperity, He will give us peace on every side, He will show us His goodness and mercy daily. He's able to do exceedingly and abundantly more than we can ever ask or think. Lord, we are putting You before all things because You are worthy. We are grateful. Blessings

336

Good Morning!

And this I pray, that your love may abound still more and more in knowledge and all discernment, [10] that you may approve the things that are excellent, that you may be sincere and without offense till the day of Christ. **Philippians 1:9-10 NKJV**

We need to strive to better understand what it means when he says Christ loved us and gave himself up for us, a fragrant offering and sacrifice to God. Here we are given not only the ground or reason why we love others but also the pattern we are to imitate as we love others. Approve is a word used for testing metal in order to find it genuine. The day of Christ will be a time of judgement, but since the recipients of the letter have a personal relationship with the Judge Himself, they need not fear eternal separation from God. Their works, however, will be judged so Paul urges that they approve and practice those things that will show them to be sincere and without offense in that day. Thank you, Lord, for blessing us to learn how to love with knowledge and discernment. We are grateful. Blessings

337

Good Morning!

Pure and undefiled religion before God and the Father is this: to visit orphans and widows in their trouble, and to keep oneself unspotted from the world.
James 1:27 NKJV

This verse is describing a pure and undefiled outward expression or demonstration of something that is inwardly true, namely of who God is and what He does. We are reminded that obedience to God is meant to be followed down to the level of every word we speak. Remember, it's difficult to practice pure and undefiled religion before our God, until we see some serious changes on the inside of ourselves. As we strive to remain unstained from the world, let's remember to look out for those who are less fortunate than we are, especially, the orphans and the widows. Thank you Lord for enough of You to share with others. Blessings

338

Good Morning!

Train up a child in the way he should go, And when he is old he will not depart from it. **Proverbs 22:6 NKJV**

Parents who raise their children in a godly manner give their children a wonderful window on what it would mean for them to choose God's way of life. Unfortunately, this verse is not a guarantee from God to parents that their children will stay in the Church if they raise them up in a godly way, but we are grateful for the early exposure to Christ. Thank you Lord for every home that is blessed to have godly parents who are raising their children in a godly way of life. We pray that when these children reach maturity they will have a better understanding of the consequences or rewards that are sure to come from the choices and decisions that they make in their lifetime. Amen. Blessings

339

Good Morning!

Why are you cast down, O my soul? And why are you disquieted within me? Hope in God; For I shall yet praise Him, The help of my countenance and my God. **Psalm 42:12 NKJV**

We have all experienced those times in our lives when we feel so alone it's difficult for us to form a positive thought. We know in our heart that God is with us, but we may feel as if we have messed up so bad that we can't trace Him. These are the times that we need to encourage ourselves. We need to tell ourselves not to be stressed because our God cares for us, we need to speak to our soul and tell ourselves not to be weary because the best way to move past misery is to remember the God of all mercies. In the midst of your despair, you must remind yourself of the hope that lies in your God, He is the lifter of your spirit. Always remember, as one trouble follows hard after another in this season and everything appears to join together for your ruin, don't forget troubles are all appointed and overruled by your Lord and Savior. We are grateful. Blessings

340

Good Morning!

For where your treasure is, there your heart will be also.
Matthew 6:21 NKJV

If something is of true value to you, there is no way for you to disguise it. The worth you place on the different things that you value in your life is evident by your priorities. The things that mean the most to you will get the majority of your time and attention. Always remember, the things that you treasure the most, will always be favored by you and they will be treated like a priceless, valuable treasure. How valuable is your relationship with God? Blessings

341

Good Morning!

For godly sorrow produces repentance leading to salvation, not to be regretted; but the sorrow of the world produces death.
2 Corinthians 7:10 NKJV

This passage of scripture shows two paths of grief. There is godly grief that produces repentance and leads to salvation. This is the type of grief that David experienced when he sinned against Bathsheba, her husband, and our God. He acknowledged his sin, grieved over it, then he eventually ran from sin to the mercy of God in salvation. Worldly grief is different. This grief may acknowledge sin, this grief may even regret or have sorrow because of the sin, but it's not sorrow because someone was hurt or because they disobeyed God. It could be sorrow over getting caught or even sorrow and sadness because of the pain the sin has caused in one's life. Worldly grief never reaches the realization that you have offended the Creator of the universe. Lord our prayer is that our grief over sin will lead us to plead for Your forgiveness, to ask for power to turn and not sin again, and a deep desire to sin less as we live with righteousness and holiness for the glory of our Lord and Savior. We are grateful. Blessings

342

Good Morning!

Wait on the Lord; Be of good courage,
And He shall strengthen your heart;
Wait, I say, on the Lord!
Psalm 27:14 NKJV

Sometimes life seems to move too slow for us or it doesn't appear to be going in the direction that we think it should. During these times, if we will just be still and ask God to position us to hear from Him, we will receive direction based on what He is desiring for us. When God calls us to wait on Him, He is asking us to delay any action on our part (get out of our own way) and pray until something happens. When we are called to wait, we should eagerly anticipate an answer. In the midst of our waiting, God is busy working things out for our good so we should be of good courage, because He's making us stronger, we should trust Him without ceasing because He is making a way out of no way, we should put all our hope in Him because He's perfecting our deliverance we should pray longer and harder because He's increasing our faith, glory! We need to confidently wait on the Lord because He is moving on our behalf we thank and praise Him because every one of His promises concerning us are yes and amen in Christ Jesus. We are forever grateful. Blessings

343

Good Morning!

Therefore, whatever you want men to do to you, do also to them, for this is the Law and the Prophets.
Matthew 7:12 NKJV

Jesus is commanding His disciples to be mindful and in every circumstance or situation to always treat people the same way you want them to treat you. If you don't speak to me me, I'll speak to you, if you don't help me in my tone of need, I'll help you in yours, if you desire to harm me or hurt me in any manner, I'll intercede for you in prayer and ask my God to forgive you. We are Christ representatives so we have to follow this command and treat all people the way we desire to be treated. Thank you Lord for being the greatest example of how we want to be treated. We are grateful. Blessings

344

Good Morning!

You will keep him in perfect peace,
Whose mind is stayed on You,
Because he trusts in You.
Isaiah 26:3 NKJV

As long as He keeps waking us up, we are going to face trouble and turmoil. So, if we trust in God and keep our mind stayed on Him, He will keep us in perfect peace because He is our everlasting rock. When everything appears to be crumbling beneath us and we don't know which way to turn, God is in the midst of working things out for our good. Our trust in Him during these times produces a peace on the inside of us that makes us want to run on and see what the end is gonna be. Thank you Lord for perfecting Your peace in us. Blessings

345

Good Morning!

but made Himself of no reputation, taking the form of a bondservant, and coming in the likeness of men. ⁸ And being found in appearance as a man, He humbled Himself and became obedient to the point of death, even the death of the cross.
Philippians 2:7-8 NKJV

Jesus came to earth to serve others. He didn't stop being God, He emptied Himself in the sense that He didn't show His unlimited powers and He didn't come as the King of Kings. Jesus was born in humility and He died in humility, His humbleness was a part of God's plan for His obedience. This is an example of how we should be humble in our obedience to Christ. Jesus went to the cross and died for us. The cross was much more than just a painful death, it was a degrading and humiliating execution. We are so thankful and so grateful for the ultimate sacrifice You made for us at the cross. Blessings

346

Good Morning!

The next day John saw Jesus coming toward him, and said, Behold! The Lamb of God who takes away the sin of the world!
John 1:29 NKJV

At times, John combines ideas to give us a broader picture to help us understand what he is trying to convey to us. We have the Lamb of God (the Passover lamb Ex. 12:3) combined with the scapegoat of the Day of Atonement (Lev. 5:16). It was the second goat (the first goat was killed on the Day of Atonement), anointed with the blood of the slain goat, that was left to die in the wilderness, bearing Israel's sin. This is where the Lamb "takes away the sin of the world" this is a reference to universal atonement. Other possible ideas John may wish to convey through the lamb metaphor are that of the lamb of the Isaac narrative in Gen. 22:8, and that of the lamb of the Suffering Servant of Is. 53:7. All of this clearly points to a sacrificial lamb. We are so thankful for the Lamb who took away the sins, our sins, of this world. Amen. Blessings

347

Good Morning!

And whatever you do, do it heartily, as to the Lord and not to men, [24]knowing that from the Lord you will receive the reward of the inheritance; for you serve the Lord Christ. **Colossians 3:23-24 NKJV**

All that we do should be done with Christ-like character, in all honesty, with intentional integrity, and with purposeful humility. We must always work heartily for our Lord, not for men. Many individuals have very little to offer others, but don't be dismayed or discouraged, you have an inheritance in waiting for you. So, continue to be faithful to God and to those He has placed over you and Jesus will give you your heavenly inheritance. Lord we are grateful for our Christ-like character. Blessings

348

Good Morning!

I will remember the works of the Lord; Surely, I will remember Your wonders of old. ^{12.} I will also meditate on all Your work And talk of Your deeds. **Psalm 77:11-12 NKJV**

We are taught to remember God's greatness, His works, His power, and His might. When we are called to different tests and trials, we need to remember how He has dealt with others in the past and most importantly how He has worked in our lives. So, let's not only remember God's deeds and His wonders, we should meditate on His goodness and His undeserved faithfulness to us. Thank you Lord for reminding us of Your goodness and how You continue to cover us in our time of need over and over and over again. We are forever grateful. Blessings

349

Good Morning!

For you, brethren, have been called to liberty; only do not use liberty as an opportunity for the flesh, but through love serve one another. **Galatians 5:13 NKJV**

In Paul's day, he envisioned three possible lifestyles, legalism and lawlessness both in of which he strongly rejected and spirit-directed living that he enthusiastically endorsed. Liberty means we have freedom from exterior rule, but this type of freedom requires new and greater responsibilities for those of us who are liberated. We as believers are no longer ruled by the law. The Holy Spirit reigns in our heart and our responsibilities are much more profound as a result of our salvation. Blessings

350

Good Morning!

Then He said to His disciples, The harvest truly is plentiful, but the laborers are few. 38. Therefore pray the Lord of the harvest to send out laborers into His harvest.
Matthew 9: 37-38 NKJV

In this scripture, the Son of God is actually saying there is a ripe harvest of spiritually lost people around us. They are hungry to know God's kingdom and they desire a good shepherd to lead them. But, rather than point them to Jesus as the Way, the Truth, and the Life, most believers don't actively reach out to share the Good News of salvation with them. Amid the chaos and uncertainty of this life, we are in need of Jesus to bring true peace to our lives. So we need to pray for more laborers of the harvest of our God. Father, please send more workers, the harvest is ripe and very plentiful. Thank you Lord. Blessings

351

Good Morning!

For everyone who asks receives, and he who seeks finds, and to him who knocks it will be opened.
Matthew 7:8 NKJV

In this verse, Jesus makes it clear that He is talking about prayer, asking from the Father, seeking from the Father, and symbolically knocking on the Father's door. We are grateful that everyone who asks of God receives an answer, everyone who seeks Him finds Him, and the door is opened to everyone who knocks. Also in this verse we see that God's responsiveness to prayer is not based on the goodness of the one who prays, but on the goodness of God. We all know that among everyone, some are unworthy but God knows that among everyone, everyone is unworthy. Lord, we thank you for Your faithfulness. Blessings

352

Good Morning!

But love your enemies, do good, and lend, hoping for nothing in return; and your reward will be great, and you will be sons of the Most High. For He is kind to the unthankful and evil. **Luke 6:35 NKJV**

Jesus? You're telling us that we need to love those whom we know are praying for our downfall? And you want us to lend to them, hoping and expecting nothing in return? Has the Holy Spirit convicted you yet? Some of us find it hard to do good for those we love, but God is saying we need to do good towards are enemies with no expectations or preconceived notions that they will do ANYTHING good for us in return. As followers of Christ, we are to give to those who will never be able to repay us, and we must remain steadfast and open in the face of their insults and persecution. Our God will reward His faithful followers. Our God "makes His sun rise on the evil and on the good, and He sends rain on the just and on the unjust" We were God's enemies, but Jesus reconciled us to God through His sacrifice (Rom. 5:10). We must be merciful because our Father is merciful. Thank You Lord for reminding me on this day, regardless of what it looks like to others, my actions are aligned with Your word and I am grateful. Blessings

353

Good Morning!

Jesus Christ is the same yesterday, today, and forever.
Hebrews 13:8 NKJV

Jesus Christ does not change and neither does His gospel. God does not change and neither does His truth (Isaiah 40:28). This doesn't mean we can't come to a better understanding. It's always good to move our beliefs closer to what God actually intended (Acts 17:11). But if a "new" teaching requires us to believe the apostles and Bible writers were mistaken, that claim is subject to the curse mentioned by Paul (1 Thessalonians 5:21). Thank You Lord for Your consistency, thank You for being the same yesterday, today, and forever. Amen. Blessings

354

Good Morning!

For I consider that the sufferings of this present time are not worthy to be compared with the glory which shall be revealed in us. **Romans 8:18 NKJV**

As God calls us to suffer in this life, we must remember the purpose behind the pain. This purpose is being worked out for those of us who are called to suffer as Christ did, by experiencing rejection, going through loneliness, and enduring hatred and negativity from the world, His glory will be revealed in us, in His time all because we choose to walk in obedience to the will of our Father. Thank you Lord for allowing the suffering. Because there is good that comes from suffering in this life. Suffering helps us to keep our eyes off the things of this world, the lust of the flesh, and the pride of life. During our time of suffering we are often inclined to lean on the Lord, to seek Him in our prayers and petitions, and to stay very close to the shelter of His loving wings. We are grateful to Him because He is with us as we experience the difficult times of this life. Blessings

355

Good Morning!

Give us this day our daily bread.
Matthew 6:11 NKJV

Our heavenly Father knows what we need. All we need to do is pursue His kingdom and righteousness, He has promised to take care of every one of our needs, one day at a time. Lord, we trust You to do what You have promised, we are grateful for the provision that is provided to us daily. Blessings

356

Good Morning!

For the LORD is good; His mercy is everlasting, And His truth endures to all generations.
Psalm 100:5 NKJV

God's faithfulness extends to all generations. Lamentations 3:23 describes this characteristic of the Lord as "great." He has never broken a promise, left a believer without His care, or failed to do all He said He would do. He has always been reliable and always will be reliable. We are so grateful to serve a God line this, thank you Lord. Amen. Blessings

Good Morning!

357

I have shown you in every way, by laboring like this, that you must support the weak. And remember the words of the Lord Jesus, that He said, 'It is more blessed to give than to receive.
Acts 20:35 NKJV

It is God and the word of His grace that builds us up and gives us an inheritance. He has blessed many of us with hands, wisdom, knowledge, and a mindset with the help of the Holy Spirit to provide for the necessities of this life. As we labor each day, we not only labor for ourselves, we are called to labor for those who are weak, those whom God has placed on our path to success. Let's not take God's goodness for granted, remember, unto much is given much is required so we must remember the truth of God, it is more blessed to give than to receive. Give of yourself, when God moves you to do so, give of your time, do this in an unselfish manner, and give of your tender, seek God first so that this giving is done under the unction of the Holy Spirit. We want all that we do to be done decently and in order. May God continue to bless those whom He has allowed to operate in the abundance of His blessings. Amen. Blessings

358

Good Morning!

For there is one God and one Mediator between God and men, the Man Christ Jesus,
1 Timothy 2:5 NKJV

As disciples of Christ, we must always pray. Our duty as Christians can be summed up in two words godliness and honesty. We are not truly honest if we are not godly and we fail to render to God what He is due. Sin has made a quarrel between us and God. Jesus is the mediator who makes peace. Those who are saved must come to the knowledge of the truth, this is God's appointed way to save sinners. If we don't know the truth, we cannot be ruled by it. Lord we thank you and we honor you for your guidance and direction in our lives. Blessings

359

Good Morning!

If My people who are called by My name will humble themselves, and pray and seek My face, and turn from their wicked ways, then I will hear from heaven, and will forgive their sin and heal their land.
II Chronicles 7:14 NKJV

When we, as God's people, humble ourselves, pray, and turn from our wicked ways, we can trust in God's promise to bring healing and restoration to our lives and the world around us. God is so faithful and He desires to bless us, heal us, guide us, restore us, teach us, uphold us, love us and show us just how much we mean to Him. We don't deserve it, but God's faithfulness and His love is unconditional. Lord we are so thankful and so grateful to have You on our side. Blessings

360

Good Morning!

The name of the Lord is a strong tower;
The righteous run to it and are safe.
Proverbs 18:10 NKJV

This is a short and simple verse, but the promise is profound and powerful. We have a Place "the name of the Lord that is always available to us. We all face times of desperation and trouble. People run to many different places looking for peace, protection, and acceptance. Some turn to the bottle as a source of comfort and joy. Some bask in their wealth and riches, others hope fame and power will provide answers during difficult times. For us, Christians, the place to run in times of trouble is straight to the name of the Lord! There is enough room, enough peace, enough safety, enough love and so much more for us all in His name. We are forever grateful. Blessings

361

Good Morning!

I beseech you therefore, brethren, by the mercies of God, that you present your bodies a living sacrifice, holy, acceptable to God, which is your reasonable service.
Romans 12:1 NKJV

God's grace and mercy is without comparison, so in the light of His amazing love towards each one of us, we are encouraged to offer our bodies, our lives, ourselves, and our very being as a living, breathing, holy sacrifice to our Savior. We are saved because of God's grace. There is nothing we can do to repay Him, but in the light of salvation's eternal glories and benefits we can offer ourselves to Him in love and gratitude, by presenting our bodies as a living sacrifice, holy, acceptable, and pleasing to God, because this is our spiritual worship. Thank you Lord, we are eternally grateful. Blessings

362

Good Morning!

Trust in the Lord forever, For in Yah, the Lord, is everlasting strength.
Isaiah 26:4 NKJV

God is perfectly able to sustain us through tribulation and to give us a peace that surpasses all understanding (Philippians 4:7)! Jesus tells us that in Him we can experience peace, strength, comfort, and so much more and this experience is everlasting for all who choose to trust in our Savior. Blessings

363

Good Morning!

But you are a chosen generation, a royal priesthood, a holy nation, His own special people, that you may proclaim the praises of Him who called you out of darkness into His marvelous light; [10] who once were not a people but are now the people of God, who had not obtained mercy but now have obtained mercy. **1 Peter 2:9-10 NKJV**

Thank you Lord for choosing us and making us Your royal priesthood, a holy nation, thank you for bringing us into the marvelous light, thank you for allowing us to be your special people so that we can proclaim praises to you. We have obtained mercy, all glory to God. We are grateful. Blessings

364

Good Morning!

The name of the Lord is a strong tower;
The righteous run to it and are safe.
Proverbs 18:10 NKJV

This is a short and simple verse, but the promise is profound and powerful. We have a Place "the name of the Lord that is always available to us. We all face times of desperation and trouble. People run to many different places looking for peace, protection, and acceptance. Some turn to the bottle as a source of comfort and joy. Some bask in their wealth and riches, others hope fame and power will provide answers during difficult times. For us, Christians, the place to run in times of trouble is straight to the name of the Lord! There is enough room, enough peace, enough safety, enough love and so much more for us all in His name. We are forever grateful. Blessings

365

Good Morning!

I beseech you therefore, brethren, by the mercies of God, that you present your bodies a living sacrifice, holy, acceptable to God, which is your reasonable service.
Romans 12:1 NKJV

God's grace and mercy is without comparison, so in the light of His amazing love towards each one of us, we are encouraged to offer our bodies, our lives, ourselves, and our very being as a living, breathing, holy sacrifice to our Savior. We are saved because of God's grace. There is nothing we can do to repay Him, but in the light of salvation's eternal glories and benefits we can offer ourselves to Him in love and gratitude, by presenting our bodies as a living sacrifice, holy, acceptable, and pleasing to God, because this is our spiritual worship. Thank you Lord, we are eternally grateful. Blessings

The End

www.ingramcontent.com/pod-product-compliance
Lightning Source LLC
LaVergne TN
LVHW020428070526
838199LV00004B/318